The Personal Trainer's Business Survival Guide

Craig S. Mastrangelo, M.S.

Exercise Science Publishing
Monterey, California
and
American Council on Exercise
San Diego, California

ISBN: 1-58518-495-0
Library of Congress Number: 2001091277

Cover design: Karen McGuire

It is not the intent of the author to diagnose or prescribe. The material contained herein is for informational purposes only. The author recommends you discuss any legal or financial matters with an attorney, accountant, or other appropriate professional.

Throughout this book, the masculine shall be deemed to include the feminine and vice versa.

To my clients, who made this book possible.

Contents

Acknowledgments

James Collins and Jerry Porras, in the acknowledgment page of their book, *Built to Last*, reference Winston Churchill when describing the process of writing a book. Mr. Churchill believed that writing a book encompasses five distinct phases: in the first phase the book is a toy or a novelty; by phase five it becomes a tyrant ruling one's life. As a small business owner I felt that my experience running a business was worth writing about to help other personal trainers interested in starting their own companies. My mind was a whirlwind of ideas and topics that I wanted to cover; Mr. Churchill would have noted that I was firmly entrenched in the first phase of book writing— the novelty phase.

I soon began to understand why writing a book is harder than actually becoming published. After the initial brainstorming sessions ran their respective courses, I was filled with a variety of prospective chapters, each with its own chapter objectives. Then came the hard part—finding the time to write diligently about each topic. This task is not easy, but is somewhat less maddening than the re-writing/editing phase because during the initial writing phase I wrote stream of consciousness and did not place too much emphasis on form or structure.

During the rewriting process, an author must face what he has written and make sense of the whole mess. Thankfully, I had a few individuals who helped make the process manageable by offering their time, professional knowledge, and editing skills. They helped prevent my creation from consuming me, and, as a result, the product has finally become what I believe to be an excellent tool for helping personal trainers start and operate successful businesses.

Many thanks to my family for accepting the idea that I could become a published author and for supporting me while I pursued my dream; to Allison and Pat Cooney, the catalysts for starting this book, without whose urging this book may well never have been written; to Andrew Burroughs for lending his time and wealth of business knowledge during the editing process; to Debbie Winstead for all her legal advice, the kind donation of her time, and for her friendship; to Brad Hawley for designing The Body Defined, Inc.'s various marketing/advertising/promotional pieces—I am indebted to you for your professional skills and kindness; to Peter Martin, a true friend, who selflessly offered his time and editing expertise.

Special thanks to my father, Clifford, who is probably second only to me in underestimating the work involved in writing this book. With each new edited version, I turned to my father, who helped give my manuscript its form and structure. Dad, thank you from the bottom of my heart for all your help!

The greatest achievement of the human spirit is to live up to one's opportunities, and make the most of one's resources.

— *Vauvenargues*

Foreword

During the last decade, personal training has become widely popular with Gold's Gym members. With this gain in popularity, personal training has also become a substantial profit center for our health clubs. Where personal training was once thought to be a service exclusively for the rich and famous, it has now matured into a profession that caters to every fitness enthusiast.

In an attempt to increase revenue, Gold's Gym has focused its attention on providing its members with personal training programs. While potentially profitable, running personal training programs requires that our health clubs focus on a variety of topics because the personal training programs become businesses within a business.

There are many obstacles to starting a personal training program. A personal training program must be able to provide excellent customer service to its clients; market itself effectively to prospective clients; maintain client referrals; overcome liability issues; implement employee policy and procedures; and provide knowledgeable trainers.

In his book, *The Personal Trainer's Business Survival Guide*, author Craig Mastrangelo has addressed business practices that a health club director or entrepreneur needs to know about starting and running a personal training business. Many business facets are discussed: the importance of trainer certification, how to set up a training company, the necessary accounting knowledge, marketing, networking, customer service, company procedures, and future growth. *The Personal Trainer's Business Survival Guide* provides insight into running a company and is a model for starting and operating a personal training business.

—Kirk Galiani
CEO, Gold's Gym International, Inc.

Success is getting what you want; happiness is wanting what you get.

— *Anonymous*

Figures

A journey of a thousand miles must begin with a single step.

— *Chinese proverb*

Getting Started

"Our doubts are traitors,

And make us lose the good we oft might win,

By fearing to attempt."

—William Shakespeare

Chapter at a Glance

Is Personal Training Right for You?
What Makes a Good Trainer?
What Makes a Good Business Owner?
Getting Started

Personal training has seen tremendous growth in recent years. Fifteen years ago, personal trainers were used almost exclusively by dedicated athletes and the rich and famous. This is not the situation today. Ordinary people are turning to trainers to assist them in their quest for physical fitness (Figure 1).

This metamorphosis has growth-related issues. Each year more people are becoming personal trainers with few restrictions on how to conduct themselves as personal trainers. Unfortunately, it is relatively easy to become a certified trainer, though certification organizations that are non-profit, such as the American Council on Exercise (ACE), National Strength and Conditioning Association (NSCA), and the American College of Sports Medicine (ACSM), are more credible, as this denotes a focus on protecting the public and providing a service to the industry as opposed to only making money. This book provides guidelines for a future trainer to follow to start a personal training business that is *profitable*, *ethical*, and *professionally credible*. This chapter focuses on issues that might help you decide whether personal training is an appropriate career choice.

Reasons people hire personal trainers:
- A person is out of shape
- A person wants to update and/or change his program
- A person is training for a specific event
- A person is coming back from an injury or prolonged illness
- A person needs motivation

Reasons clients retain the services of a personal trainer:
- Improved flexibility
- Increased muscular strength
- Improved overall lifestyle
- Improve self-confidence/self-esteem
- Improve emotional/psychological health

Figure 1

Is Personal Training Right for You?

"A man can succeed at almost anything for which he has unlimited enthusiasm."

—Charles M. Schwab

Whether you are a college graduate, a certified trainer, or just seeking a career change, personal training is a job that may bring much satisfaction. Say goodbye to romantic visions. While contemplating personal training as a career, investigate the positives this profession has to offer, and consider some of the negative aspects as well.

Benefits of the Personal Training Industry

Independent trainers are their own bosses (see Chapter 3). They work flexible work hours, their business expenses are tax deductible, work attire is casual, and they have the opportunity to meet a variety of people. These "perks" make personal training very appealing. There are few professions that have all these advantages. In addition, personal trainers are educators who teach the benefits of a healthy lifestyle.

Is this the right profession for you? Are you convinced that you should start your own personal training business? Before answering these questions, let's examine some of the negative aspects associated with this profession.

Drawbacks of the Personal Training Industry

Personal training, once considered a privilege accessible only to the rich and famous, is not always a glamorous profession. While work hour flexibility is most certainly a benefit, there are two important factors to consider: 1) Appointments must be carefully scheduled in order to generate income; (if a trainer is not working, he is not getting paid—unless the trainer has others working for him); and 2) Trainers are most in demand during what the working public thinks of as "off-hours": Clients request training sessions as early as 5 or 6 a.m., or as late as 9 or 10 p.m.

It is not uncommon for a new personal trainer to work early in the morning and then have no appointments until the evening. If you use this free time wisely, you can make the business expand and grow more profitable. Conversely, if you do not spend your time productively, your business may remain a less profitable "one-person" operation. The true entrepreneur thinks ahead and plans for the future.

What Makes a Good Trainer?

"Never mind what business you are in—what are you good at?"

—Selling the Invisible, *by Harry Beckworth*

Before deciding on personal training as a career, critically assess your skills and abilities. A personal trainer must be a good communicator, an effective handler of responsibility and conflict, and must *always be on time!* Punctuality cannot be overemphasized. No matter how personable you are or how many certifications you have, no matter what celebrities you have trained, you will not be hired if you are not on time. *You will not make it in this industry if you are not punctual!* Some trainers like to joke that half the battle (and half the job responsibility) is showing up on time. Punctuality shows the paying clientele respect and creates rapport between the client and trainer.

What Makes a Good Business Owner?

"I have concentrated all along on building the finest retailing company that we possibly could. Period. Creating a huge personal fortune was never particularly a goal of mine."

—Sam Walton, Founder, Wal-Mart

There is a difference between becoming a successful personal trainer and becoming a successful business owner. In addition to possessing all of the competencies of a personal trainer, you will need management skills and a broader vision. See Figure 2 for a list of qualities essential for any business owner.

Getting Started

"Putting profits after people and products was magical at Ford."

—Don Peterson, Former CEO, Ford, 1994

If you believe you have the personality and the temperament, congratulations! These personality traits will set you apart from other trainers.

Traits of a successful business owner

1. Sets and shares a vision
2. Focuses on customers first
3. Develops and supports team- and group-building dynamics
4. Solves problems and makes decisions
5. Manages people: club owner(s), club members, and clients
6. Manages time, resources, and projects
7. Takes initiative beyond the job description
8. Displays professional ethics
9. Anticipates and manages change
10. Shares information
11. Manages business processes
12. Displays technical skills
13. Handles emotions
14. Shows compassion
15. Leads by example

Figure 2

However, a word of caution: Merely being personable, on time, and responsible does not necessarily mean you are ready to start your own personal training business. Most trainers overlook one additional and necessary step because they are eager to start making money. They often sacrifice quality in order to make a quick buck.

What differentiates successful trainers from their competition? In a word, certification. While certification is not a legal requirement to start a personal training business, it makes you more credible and marketable. To make a positive, lasting impression and improve future marketability, it is important you increase your knowledge base beyond a single certification course. Productive paths to follow in this pursuit include a few college courses in nutrition, physiology, biomechanics, sports medicine, and weight training. Another way to learn valuable information while gaining hands-on experience is to work as an assistant or intern in a health club or therapy clinic. Such experience will help you better understand and deal with the demands and questions you will face.

Recommended credentials for a successful personal training business owner

1. Degree in exercise science or equivalent
2. Minimum of six months of quality experience designing and implementing exercise programs
3. Certification from a nationally recognized fitness certification organization
4. Professional liability insurance
5. Quality references

Figure 3

James Collins and Jerry Porras, in their book *Built to Last: Successful Habits of Visionary Companies* (1997), note that "most companies benefit from articulating both core values and purpose in their core ideology" (p.78). If prospective trainers present their clientele with a superior product, profits will inevitably follow.

Good personal trainers must be very professional and keenly focused on customer service. This book provides you with the fundamentals of starting and operating a profitable business. See Figure 3 for a list of recommended credentials before opening your own personal trainer business.

Reference

Collins, J.C. and Porras, J.I. (1997). Built to Last: *Successful Habits of Visionary Companies*. New York. Harper Collins Books.

## 2

Certification

"There can be no friendship without confidence,

and no confidence without integrity."

—*Samuel Johnson*

Chapter at a Glance

The Competition
The Importance of Certification
Costs
Tax Deductions
CPR
Personal Training Licenses

The Competition

The more a company resembles its competition, the less reason it gives a client to choose its services. Without proper credentials, a trainer can go only so far. Certifications, continuing education, and extracurricular work experience enhance the services provided by a personal trainer. With each certification and continuing education credit, you distinguish yourself from your competitors. Degrees in exercise science as well as personal training certifications breed instant credibility. If a company decides to train its clients with trainers who do not possess the necessary certifications or degrees, that company will never achieve its optimum potential.

The Importance of Certification

A personal training business cannot exist without clients. Prospective clients generally seek out those trainers who are most qualified and knowledgeable. Personal training, like any other service-oriented profession, is based on relationships. Chapter 1 addressed the fact that not all prospective trainers become certified before starting their own businesses. This could be a costly mistake. Certifications enhance a company's credibility by providing industry guidelines, which, in turn, appeal to the medical community of doctors, physical therapists, orthopedists, chiropractors, etc. Perhaps most importantly, being certified demonstrates to the public that you have a certain level of competence, proven by your ability to apply your knowledge and skills.

More and more health care providers are recognizing the importance of qualified personal trainers for post-rehabilitative and post-surgical care. The requisite knowledge for some (not all) certification associations does not require personal trainers to deal with anyone other than the "apparently healthy adult." Health care providers know this, so as a trainer you need to be properly certified to build more professional relationships with these medical providers. Networking with the medical community will be covered in Chapter 9.

In the beginning, you should acquire knowledge that will prepare you to work with specific populations. There are numerous national certifications to pursue. When researching certification associations, seek out those that are credible. The situations presented during the test will most likely be similar to the ones a trainer will face in real life. Certifications assess personal trainer's ability to interact with people, which is a huge part of this profession. By choosing a reputable certification association, you place professionalism and customer service ahead of all other objectives (Appendix A).

Costs

There is no single certification association, and so, there is no standard fee. The cost of certification can range from $100 to $1000. A majority of the more expensive certification associations also offer educational seminars prior to the exam. If you do not have a degree in a related field, it is probably in your best interest to obtain a certification from one of the associations that offer such seminars. Seminars offer the opportunity to ask questions, solidify knowledge, and learn in a hands-on environment. Additionally, you can improve your interpersonal skills and become acquainted with your future peers (and quite possibly, future competitors).

Tax Deductions

Business-related costs are tax deductible. Materials purchased to improve one's knowledge, certification exams, and other related business expenses are all tax deductible. Taxes and deductions will be covered in detail in Chapter 5. Tax deductions are very useful to small business owners, but failure to understand some basic business tenets may be the difference between a successful company and one that goes bankrupt.

Moral of the story: Do not overestimate the importance of the tax break. A penny spent is not a penny earned!

CPR

Being certified in Cardiopulmonary Resuscitation (CPR) is a prerequisite to join most national personal training certification associations, including ACE. Trainers must be prepared for any and all situations, especially those that could be life threatening. Some insurance carriers require that trainers possess CPR certification before they will consider granting liability coverage. Local YMCA and American Red Cross chapters offer classes and testing.

Personal Training Licenses

The personal training industry is self-regulated and lacks standardization. Anyone can consider him or herself a trainer, even without credentials. To date, no state government has enacted licensing laws. Physical therapists, massage therapists, doctors, etc., all must have state licensing before they can practice. While many certifications encompass similar material, be sure to choose one that follows accepted certification practices and adheres to current industry guidelines and standards. For this reason, it is important that you choose a well-respected and recognized certification agency (Appendix A).

Independent Contractor vs. Employee

## 3

Independent Contractor

A person who performs services for another person or business under an expressed or implied agreement and who is not subject to the owner's control or right to control the manner and the means by which the services are performed. The owner is therefore not responsible for the acts or omissions or the insurance of the independent contractor.

Employee

A person who works for another person in exchange for financial compensation. An employee complies by the instructions and directions of their employer and reports to them on a regular basis.

Chapter at a Glance

Advantages and Disadvantages of Being
an Employee

Advantages and Disadvantages of Being
an Independent Contractor

Approaching Health Clubs

Consulting Legal Counsel

Personal trainers must decide whether they want to be hired as employees or agree to become contractors. While there are valid arguments for both employee and contractor status, both the business owner and the personal trainer must understand the ramifications of their decisions. What is most important, regardless of which status is chosen, is to declare this status to avoid difficulties with the Internal Revenue Service (IRS).

An individual's status as either a contractor or employee is an important issue because each has its own series of tax considerations. The IRS determines whether an individual is an employee or contractor based on specific guidelines. These guidelines attempt to determine which party (employer or contractor) has "control." Control is generally defined by the following list of criteria: method of payment, work hours, length of professional relationship, expense reimbursement, and the ability of a personal trainer to work for more than one business owner.

Trainers should speak with a lawyer or an accountant when deciding which title to carry. It is important for personal trainers to determine their classification as either employees or contractors.

Advantages and Disadvantages of Being an Employee

In the early stages of their personal training careers, most trainers do not have the educational background, experience, or capital to venture out on their own. So they work at health clubs or private exercise studios. There are benefits to being an employee. However, the purpose of this book is to provide personal trainers a working knowledge of how they can begin their own business.

Advantages and Disadvantages of Being an Employee

Advantages

- Insurance coverage
- Pension plans
- Paid vacation time
- Guaranteed wages (income)
- Job security (if performance is satisfactory)

Disadvantages

- Fixed income
- Limitations in job growth
- Employment often restricted to one employer

Figure 4

You can gain much practical experience working as an employee. This background training will be very useful to novice personal trainers. The advantages and disadvantages of being an employee are listed in Figure 4.

Advantages and Disadvantages of Being an Independent Contractor

Working as a contractor results in some additional administrative responsibilities. You not only have your main job to perform (personal training), but must also keep track of items such as payroll, taxable income, and business expenses. Being a contractor (one's own boss) is manageable and may be more rewarding than being an employee. The advantages and disadvantages of being a contractor are listed in Figure 5.

It is important to note that even though you may be considered a consultant with a company, you can still pay yourself a salary out of business (sole proprietorship, corporation) revenue. This is standard procedure and is endorsed by the IRS. However, no business owner should simply write a check anytime he or she feels like it.

Advantages and Disadvantages of Being an Independent Contractor

Advantages

- More control over business practices and decision making
- Flexibility in scheduling
- Tax-deductible expenses
- Freedom to work on a variety of projects
- Potential for higher income
- Being your own boss

Disadvantages

- Necessity and cost of liability coverage
- Increased accountability and liability
- Less job security
- Paying one's own taxes
- No Workmen's Compensation benefits in the event of injury

Figure 5

Approaching Health Clubs

Trainers who want to work for themselves, but not invest a tremendous amount of capital into a private studio, can utilize existing health clubs as possible business sites. Health clubs can either maintain an "in-house" training department, or they can outsource the responsibilities to contractors. Such contractual arrangements are low-cost alternatives to starting new personal training businesses.

Before approaching a health club about contracting space, first determine the costs of doing business at such a location. Although a pre-existing health club is a low-cost alternative to providing one's own training facility, you will still incur costs. It is important to determine what these costs are going to be and to estimate the income that can be generated at an existing location. Is your business going to have exclusive personal training rights at the health club, or are there going to be a number of competitors using the site and competing for the same prospects? How many employees is your company going to have? How many clients can your company train per week? Based on this information, a business owner must establish a pricing structure that is competitive, but also provides a profitable wage.

Some health clubs are open to outsourcing the responsibilities of a personal training department because it frees up administrative time and saves them money. However, to convince a health club that your company can provide its members with quality personal training, you must present them with a business plan detailing your expected growth. You should also include a brief biography of each employee (highlighting his or her education and certifications) and proof of insurance.

Not every health club is open to the idea of outsourcing its personal training department. Take your time when considering which avenue to pursue. Opening your own studio is more expensive but gives you greater control. Providing contracted training for a health club involves almost zero overhead, but you end up having no say in decision-making processes. Fully explore both options on paper before deciding which avenue to pursue.

Consulting Legal Counsel

Before signing a consulting contract with any company, hire an attorney to review the contract. Additionally, have the attorney develop an Independent Contractor Agreement for your business (Appendix B). And make sure that any agreement or contract developed for your use is enforceable in the state(s) where your business operates.

Setting Up Your Company

## 4

"Forewarned is forearmed."

—*Anonymous*

"Ignorance is not bliss—it is oblivion."

—*Generation of Vipers,*

by Philip Wylie

Chapter at a Glance

The Mission Statement

The Business Plan

Forming Your Company

The Mission Statement

Businesses should not open their doors until they define the reasons they are in business. A mission statement tells your clients the goals and beliefs that build the foundation of your business, and helps them decide whether your business is suitable for their individual needs. The mission statement is a way to differentiate your business from the competition. Remember to be as clear and succinct as possible in communicating exactly what service you will be providing your customers (Figure 6).

Sample Mission Statement

Our company is dedicated to meeting your fitness needs by providing one-to-one personal training to help you maximize your results!

Figure 6

The Business Plan

"The ancestor of every action is a thought." —*Ralph Waldo Emerson*

The business plan lays the foundation for a successful business. From a company's philosophy to its daily business procedures, this document helps keep a business on track, growing, and profitable. The time (weeks, if not months) it takes to put together a Business Plan is time well spent. Each section of the plan must be carefully researched, defined, and clearly stated. A detailed and honest business plan can be the difference between success and failure. In developing a business plan, do not sugarcoat any areas of concern. Something perceived to be an obstacle or problem now will most likely still be present months and years down the road.

Components of a Successful Business Plan

As tempting as it may be to gloss over some aspects of a business plan, do not do it. The fact that others are working as trainers and earning money does not mean that any individual can simply make up some business cards and start his own company. There are certain components that must be included in the business plan that will clarify a company's immediate *viability* and future *profitability.*

Figure 7 outlines the required components of a detailed and complete Business Plan. An example of a business plan can also be found in Appendix C.

Components of a Business Plan

Executive Summary—A synopsis of the major factors that will help make a company successful in a competitive market.

Company Description—An overview of the elements (nature of the business, distinctive competence, etc.) of the company.

Market Analysis—An identification of the industry and its current and future outlook, the company's target markets, and the competition.

Marketing and Sales Activities—A description of how the business will market and promote itself.

Company's Services—A description of how the company is going to satisfy the needs of the marketplace.

Operations—A description of how the company will conduct business (rent a space or work as contractor in existing location). Also, a list of the company's competitive advantages (experience, techniques, etc.).

Management and Ownership—A description of management's skills, talent, and expertise. Also, a description of the type of legal entity (sole proprietorship, partnership, or corporation).

Funds Required—An outline of the current funding requirements and the use of these funds.

Financial Data—A financial description of all information covered in the various sections of the business plan. It will detail budgeting, forecasting, projections, past financial information (if applicable), and the name of accountant/bookkeeper (if applicable).

Appendices—A compilation of other information that is relevant to the company (especially relevant to potential investors). This information might include resumes of key managers, professional references, market studies, and pertinent published material.

Figure 7

Forming Your Company

Starting a company can be relatively easy. To be considered a business, one must file either one's name or the company name—considered a "Doing Business As" (DBA)—with the local county office. This process accomplishes two things: 1) It provides government recognition of the new business, and 2) It allows the business owner to research whether another company has previously registered this chosen name. Researching the use of a business name is crucial when starting a business. If you fail to research the availability of a chosen name and conduct business with a name already registered by another company, you may be subject to legal action by the other company. While there are exceptions to this rule (e.g., service products versus tangible products), it is best to register a name that has not previously been used. Doing so decreases the chances that someone is using the same name nationally. This is typically the only step for businesses that are *sole proprietorships.*

Choosing a Business Entity

There are a few different choices available to a business owner once he decides on starting his own business. Each choice has its own benefits and drawbacks. Listed below are descriptions of some common types of business entities.

Sole Proprietorship

A *sole proprietorship* is the simplest form of business. A sole proprietorship is owned and operated by a single individual. The sole owner and the business are not separate entities. A sole proprietorship is easy to form and has very low start-up costs. There are no business taxes, division of profits, organizational fees, annual licensing fees, or annual reporting requirements. One person, the owner, makes business decisions. When considering the company's size and financial limitations during start-up, it is not necessary to incorporate the company while it is in its infancy stage. Once it grows and begins to take on employees or contractors, the issue of liability becomes more important. At this stage, it is advisable to seek legal advice on the issue of incorporation.

A sole proprietorship has some disadvantages. The owner (sole proprietor) is personally responsible for any debts or liabilities incurred by the business. An individual's current and future earnings may be subject to the debts and liabilities of the business. The business is service oriented and, as such, the entrepreneur needs to be professional and attentive to every aspect of his business. Failure to do so can result in debt accumulation or lawsuits, for which the owner is personally liable. Being professional and paying heed to what needs to be done to run a successful business will prevent such unfortunate situations from arising.

Partnership

A *partnership* is an association of two or more persons who have agreed to co-own and operate a business for profit. Forming a partnership is easy. The start-up costs are low; there is an exemption from business taxes; decisions can be brainstormed by co-owners; and having more than one owner increases the company's assets—making more capital available.

However, many entrepreneurs overlook the importance of good partner selection before launching a venture. Soured business relationships usually prevent a company from attaining its full potential. Before entering into a partnership with someone, research the individual's work ethic, trustworthiness, past employment performances, and business philosophy. Once the decision has been made to enter into a partnership, hire a lawyer to draft documents that highlight responsibilities, partners' roles, and "out clauses" (whether they are buy-out or dropout) that detail what each partner needs to do, and is entitled to, should either situation arise.

Corporation

A *corporation* is defined as a business operating as an independent legal entity. By being separate from the owners, a corporation protects owners' personal assets from liability. Proprietorships have finite growth and size potential; a corporation generally has unlimited growth and size potential.

Owners must be very careful about the protection of personal assets provided by the establishment of a corporation. This "shield" of protection is not 100%. If a company is managed with an owner's personal interests in mind rather than the company's (e.g., fraud), the owners may be accused of "piercing the corporate veil." If a company and its owners are sued for such practices, they cannot hide behind the corporate shield; thus their own personal assets may be in jeopardy (decided upon by a court of law). Other disadvantages to forming a corporation are higher cost, complicated setup, and extensive government regulation.

Establishing Business Policies

New businesses must not only have a mission statement and business plan, but must also consider the importance of establishing business policies. These policies should define how a business will develop and enforce its operational rules. As members of a service-oriented industry, personal trainers will be involved in human conflict. When clients know your policies and procedures, there is less chance for conflict or debate to arise.

Important items to cover with clients include your company's cancellation, no-show, and late policies. Anticipating these issues and establishing policies to deal with them enable the business owner to run a company more efficiently and productively. Making policy and procedure decisions "on the fly" may anger clients due to perceived inconsistencies in the services being provided. Do not fall into this trap. Companies limit their opportunity for growth and success if they do not give attention to business policies.

Your company's policies should be covered with each new client, be presented in writing, and signed by you and the client. Notice of cancellation requirements; the method; term, and form of payment expected; expectations regarding workout apparel; and business hours are the "basics" that should be discussed. This allows any potential conflicts to be handled professionally and amicably. These same policies can be incorporated into a company's Personal Training Agreement (Appendix D). By reading and signing this agreement, the client acknowledges that he understands the policies and procedures and agrees to abide by them.

To instill trust and confidence, make sure your clients read the Personal Training Agreement as soon as possible. If clients identify potential areas of conflict, they will assume that there are more such items hidden in the agreement. Do not play games with clients and do not try to hide any company policy or procedure. Most clients recognize that a business needs to enforce certain rules and regulations to ensure proper function. Clients feel better hearing about policies from a company representative, rather than reading the small type of a personal training agreement.

Session Rates

On the issue of pricing, think of the old adage: "Charge what the market will bear." If people are willing to pay a certain dollar value for personal training services, a business might as well charge them the market rate. In reality, the price charged is going to be a combination of many things.

When deciding on a pricing schedule, closely examine three areas of concern:

1. How competitive is your pricing as compared to that of other personal training companies in your area?
2. Are your company's fees based on personal training experience and credentials?
3. Is your company achieving its financial goals under its current fee structure?

Too often, trainers starting a business formulate their pricing schedule based solely on the "average" fees charged by the competition in their geographic area. This is a good first step, but as a business owner you must investigate further to determine how many sessions at this "hypothetical" price you would need to conduct per week to cover expenses and make a *profit.*

To determine how much to charge (Figure 8), as the business owner you must take into account your weekly or monthly expenses (costs). These costs can be *variable* (e.g., printing supplies, meals, travel, gas, parking,

Determining Training Fees

Let's say that you train six clients per day (120 sessions/month) and each session is one hour in length. You charges $50 per session so your daily total is $300 and the weekly summation is $1500. After business expenses, of say $500 (33%), you are left with $1,000. You can either pay yourself or put the money back into the promotion of the company.

Suppose you desire a personal income of more than $4,000 per month ($1,000 x 4= $4,000). How much more do you need to charge for each "session hour" to make $5,000 per month? If you charge $62.50 per session and train six clients per day, your daily total will be $375 and your weekly summarization will be $1875. If you train the same 120 sessions per month, after your hypothetical expenses (33%), you will be left with $5,025. So, to raise your personal income $1,025 per month (assuming expenses stay fixed at 33%), you must increase the individual session fee by $12.50.

The question is: Will the market bear such an increase?

Figure 8

vehicle repair, merchant's accounts, etc.) or they can be *fixed* (rent, telephone, pager, equipment, insurance, etc.). Determine the *break-even* point and then increase this number to cover standard of living expenses. Making a profit does not simply mean covering all of the incoming business bills; it also means paying yourself!

Determine how your credentials and experience should factor into your pricing schedule. Trainers who have a degree, a few years of experience, or other marketable abilities have a better chance of charging higher prices than their "geographical" competitors. Do not assume, however, that someone who has a master's degree, and is training clients in Nebraska, is going to be able to command the same training fee as a trainer with a master's degree training clients in Los Angeles or New York City. Market demographics heavily influence pricing. Personal trainers may feel they deserve certain training fees, but if their prospective clients disagree, or the market cannot sustain such prices, they will have difficulty meeting their business plan objectives. Be reasonable when deciding on pricing strategy. Do not make the issue too personal. Ultimately, pricing comes down to what a company's target market is willing to pay.

Business Records

Personal training is a business, and close attention must be paid to financial records. An understanding of the financial aspect of a business is extremely important. You must know how to budget, prepare reports, and track costs in order to successfully run a business.

Learning and becoming proficient in this area of business is vital to the success and future growth of your company (see Chapter 5).

Personal Liability Documents

When you meet with prospective clients during initial consultations, it is important that you learn as much about them as possible. Areas of concern are listed below (see Appendix E for an example of a Health History Questionnaire):

- *General Information* (name, address, physician, person to contact in case of emergency, etc.)
- *Personal Health History* (Risk Factor Assessment)
- *Exercise History*
- *Smoking History*
- *Nutrition History*
- *Family History*

Make sure the questionnaire is easy to complete yet asks for all the necessary health-related information. This will help you provide the client with a targeted, goal-oriented program, while screening for any risk factors that may limit the training program (e.g., asthma, recent heart attack, high cholesterol). After screening for these risk factors, you may require a Medical Clearance Form (Appendix F) from the client prior to starting a fitness program.

Requiring a medical release allows the client's physician to note any special restrictions the patient may have, or any modifications that should be incorporated into the personal training program. Unfortunately, doctors too often view these releases as an assumption of liability should any injury occur with their patient. If a doctor refuses to sign a medical release form, make a phone call to let the doctor know that you merely want the doctor's professional opinion and exercise parameters regarding the conditions cited by the client on the Health History Questionnaire.

You can also request a client's medical records regarding a specific condition using a Release of Information Form (Appendix G). Requests for medical records occur infrequently and are generally related to a need for more concrete knowledge regarding a specific condition (beyond what a physician has written on a medical release). These release forms are rarely used. If you have a problem obtaining information from a doctor, you should not use a client's permission to obtain these records as a way of circumventing the doctor's orders. The reason for this is very straightforward: Regardless of a personal trainer's knowledge of said condition, a physician's, orthopedist's, or physical therapist's base of knowledge is usually more comprehensive than that of a trainer (unless you have a background in a related field). Always establish professional relationships with the medical community because, as Chapter 9 will point out, these relationships are a great source of referral business.

Always have clients sign a Full Disclosure of Physical Condition/Informed Consent and Assumption of Risk and Release of Liability prior to training (Appendix H). Requirements for these forms vary by state. By signing these documents, a client acknowledges the risks associated with exercise programs and gives consent. However, clients are not signing off or waiving their rights with regard to *negligence* (see Chapter 6). Release of liability and informed consent forms absolve the trainer from liability if the client errs. However, trainer *negligence* is not protected under any documentation. For more information regarding negligence, consult legal counsel.

Obtaining Insurance

Getting proper insurance coverage is extremely important. If your company is ever sued, suffers theft, or loses property due to fire, you will be glad you devoted some time to learning how best to protect your business.

The best way to learn about the kinds of insurance you will need is to speak directly to insurance agents or brokers. To find the right agent, make sure he or she is licensed in the state in which your company will be doing business. Find out how many current clients are in the health and fitness industry. If the agent is unfamiliar with health and fitness protection, find another agent who has experience in this field.

Many professional organizations such as ACE, together with local agencies, provide coverage to some, if not all, the areas noted in Figure 9. To

Areas of Insurance
- Property Insurance
- Business Interruption Coverage
- General Liability
- Professional Liability
- Disability
- Insurance as an Independent Contractor

Figure 9

determine which agencies provide the most comprehensive coverage, request additional information via mail. The cost of coverage may vary, so it is important to research the costs! Diligent research can save your company substantial money.

Choosing a Business Name and Logo

Choosing a business name and creating a logo requires time and thought. Each serves to identify a business and to distinguish its products and services from those of competitors. The name ultimately chosen should describe what services the company provides. Beware of creating a business name that is too specific. Such a name could negatively affect expansion of your services in the future. For example, naming a company "John Smith's Personal Training Studios" may not be appropriate. At a future date, Mr. Smith might decide to add aerobics classes or post-rehabilitation services, and his company name may not provide the necessary marketing image to the public. To prepare for future growth, a better name for the above example would be "John Smith's Health and Fitness Studios." Clearly, the type of service the studio offers is implicit, yet the types of services provided (chiropractic, nutritional, post-rehab, etc.) are unlimited.

A company logo should mesh well with the business name. The reason is simple: Every piece of printed material will contain both the company name and its logo. If you lack artistic ability, hire a graphics designer to create a company name, design a logo, and develop a company letterhead. The initial cost may be more than you planned to spend, but remember the old saying: *"You never get a second chance to make a first impression."* Product name and logo are powerful marketing tools.

Corporate Example

Nike is an example of how global marketing tactics have helped increase public awareness of its sports apparel company. As public awareness of the products they offer has increased, Nike no longer prints the company name on its merchandise. It simply prints the Swoosh Design®. People not only recognize which company the Swoosh Design represents, they also equate quality with these products.

Companies do change their name and logo for a variety of reasons (mergers, bankruptcies, etc.), though the occurrence for small businesses is rare. The reproduction costs are not justified when a company is in its infancy. Make sure the name and logo present an appropriate consumer image before you invest money in printed materials.

Trademarks

When establishing a "trade name" (a name used for legal and banking matters), a company has the opportunity to legally protect its name from competitors. Company names and logos are considered "intellectual property" and are often protected by laws against unfair competition.

The fitness industry is service-oriented. Therefore, the legal symbol to identify a company's services is a service mark, not a trademark. A service mark distinguishes a company's service from that of other companies. However, it is just as important to obtain a trademark for your business if you want to protect your company's name and logo. Consult a trademark lawyer on how best to protect the financial and "intellectual" interests of a company.

Business Checking Accounts

One of the first tasks to complete after selecting a company name is to open a business checking account. The name of the account will be under the company's "trade name." Therefore, documentation regarding authenticity will be required by the banks. Compare the services offered by several establishments, as there are a variety of monthly and annual fees that accompany corporate bank accounts. Establish an account with a bank that will offer you the lowest fees with the greatest opportunity for future professional relationships (e.g., loans).

Bank accounts allow a business owner to pay for business expenses with "company money." New business owners should not "dip" into these funds unless it is absolutely necessary. Any money taken from the business checking account must be detailed for tax reasons. The best course of action is to open an account, pay for business expenses with a business checking account, and pay salaries based on the revenue generated by personal training. If you borrow from your business, make sure a written promissory note is executed.

Accountants and Payroll Companies

Once a company is generating income and expenses, an accountant may be needed. Chapter 5 will cover in greater detail the importance of hiring an accountant. Once a company is able to hire employees, it may also require the services of a payroll company. There are payroll companies that will accept small businesses with as few as one employee. Hiring a payroll company relieves a business from a lot of tedious paperwork. This is not to say that a business owner should not handle his or her own payroll. However, it is wise to assess whether the amount of time and energy spent on preparing the payroll could be better spent on other aspects of the company. Contact a few payroll companies, obtain competitive bids, and compare their services. Some payroll companies may charge their clients a "reasonable" fee if a business terminates their agreement. Be sure you understand what "reasonable" entails.

A payroll company is a valuable asset to the small business owner. It prepares a company's payroll and files payroll taxes, quarterly taxes, annual taxes, and all paperwork associated with a company's payroll processing. In addition, a payroll company is liable for its mistakes, thereby protecting you from legal problems.

Merchant Accounts

Thus far, this chapter has discussed the professional and legal details of starting a business. However, not every detail must be adopted for a business to be professional and successful. Such is the case with merchant accounts, which allow a business to accept credit cards. In order for a company to accept credit cards, it must complete a bank application form. Be forewarned, however, that banks are reluctant to open credit card merchant's accounts for new, non-retail businesses. There are a few requirements that must be met before a bank will grant a business a merchant account. To qualify, business owners typically must have a storefront to their business location. The bank will usually send a representative to survey the business location. Another criterion that banks use when considering an application is the length of time a company has been in business. Some banks will not consider an application unless the company has existed for at least one year.

A personal training company should develop a professional relationship with a local bank as soon as the company opens its doors. While a bank may be hesitant to give a loan or open a merchant account to a company it does not know, chances will be greatly enhanced if the company has already established a professional relationship with a bank's representative.

Prospective buyers have a tendency to use credit cards because such purchases are easy. Accepting credit cards has two major benefits: 1) It is less time consuming for the client, and 2) It automatically adds credibility to a company. Accepting credit cards enhances the image of professionalism. Remember, a large percentage of the service industry is based on perception. Prospective clients may negatively prejudge a company that does not accept credit cards, even if it has great trainers.

The cost may vary, but the typical cost of electronic credit card terminals is $500–$1,000. If this is too expensive, speak with a bank about the possibility of leasing the units (charges can range from $30 – $60 monthly). The final cost incurred by the merchant account holder is a fixed percentage of each charged sale. If a company owns or leases an electronic credit card terminal, the percentage charged will be *significantly* lower (0.75%– 2% of the total sale). If a company processes charge slips via the "paper" method (owner must process all the charge slips and personally deposit them at bank) the fee is higher (2%–5% of the total sale).

In summary, if a company can afford the additional expense, obtaining a merchant account is a valuable customer service tool.

Company Uniform

A company uniform promotes professionalism. Few prospective clients will be impressed with a trainer who wears a nondescript T-shirt and shorts, regardless of how qualified or knowledgeable that trainer may be. It is important for a business owner to run his business with integrity and *professionalism.* Wearing company clothing presents the business owner and his employees in a neat, professional manner and enhances the credibility of a company. It is also a great way to advertise your business. When you or one of your employees are training a client, you are advertising your company to potential future clients.

To purchase shirts with company logos, look in the Yellow Pages under T-shirts or uniforms.

Another Source of Revenue

Selling company clothing can be another income source, once you have established yourself and can afford the up-front fee associated with clothing purchases (clothing often must be ordered in predetermined quantities).

Business Phone and Pager

Having both a business phone line and a pager is not necessary if you are working for yourself. However, having a pager or cell phone with voice mail is vital from day one. These will allow you and your trainers to receive calls from clientele and prospective clients 24 hours a day, 7 days a week. Voice mail eliminates the need to check an answering machine to determine if any calls were received while you were unavailable. If a client calls to cancel an appointment using voice mail, you can adjust your schedule accordingly.

Once your company becomes established, a business phone line should be installed. This allows trainers to call prospective clients and have them call the company without having to leave messages with an automated device (pager).

Final Thought

Earlier in this chapter, your company's pricing structure was discussed. When starting a personal training company, determine the start-up costs, fixed costs, variable costs, personal income, and how many personal training sessions the company can expect to conduct. Once these estimations have been calculated, you can draft a pricing structure that reflects all of these costs and, if all goes well, allows the company to operate comfortably in the "black."

Suggested Readings

Abrams, R.M. (1993). *The Successful Business Plan: Secrets and Strategies,* 2nd ed. Grants Pass, Oregon. The Oasis Press/PSI Research.

Hardwicke, J.W. and Emerson, R.W. (1992). *Business Law,* 2nd ed. New York. Barron's Business Review Series.

Resources

U.S. Patent and Trademark Office (PTO)
U.S. Department of Commerce
Washington, D.C. 20231
www.uspto.gov

Trademark Assistance Center: 703.308.9000

International Trademark Association
1133 Avenue of the Americas
New York, New York 10036
212.768.9887
www.inta.org

## 5

Accounting and Bookkeeping

"Anticipate that costs will go up; interest rates will go up; it will take longer than planned for construction. Everything costs more and takes longer than planned. Things go wrong. Assume you've underestimated all costs and build in a cushion. Use a good accountant or bookkeeper, and a good lawyer, and listen to their advice. Get help in those areas in which you aren't familiar."

—*Martha Johnson, Owner, Supper Restaurant*

Chapter at a Glance

Financial Definitions
Financial Forecasts
Hiring a Bookkeeper and Accountant
Measuring Profitability
Payment Programs
Hiring a Billing Company
Hiring a Payroll Company

Financial Definitions

Following is a list of financial definitions that will help you determine your current financial status, develop projections, and prepare reports.

Current Assets:	Assets that are easily liquidated.
Capital:	The net worth of a company's assets.
Fixed Costs:	Expenses that must be paid regardless of a company's revenues (e.g., rent, utilities, phone bills, insurance, etc.).
Variable Costs:	Costs that vary depending on the level of production (e.g., the amount of resistance tubing purchased for a boot camp will vary depending on the number of class participants).
Break-Even Analysis:	Total expenditures equal total revenues.
Cost Allocation:	The percentage of company expenses (rent, electricity bill, marketing, etc.) allocated to each program or division to allow accurate expense accounting.
Working Capital:	The ability of a company to meet its financial obligations.
Current Expenditures:	Short-term expenditures that are completely charged to income in the year they occur.
Depreciation:	A deduction method to recover cost of property over its useful life.
Current Liabilities:	Debts due within one year.
Long-Term Liabilities:	Debts not payable within the next 12 months.
Accounts Receivable:	Monies owed to the company for services rendered.
Accounts Payable:	Monies owed by the business.

Financial Forecasts

"A penny saved is a penny earned." — *Benjamin Franklin*

The previous chapter addressed some of the start-up costs, fixed costs, and variable costs facing the small business owner. Almost everything has a cost attached to it. A weekly advertisement in a newspaper has a cost. If you decide to hire additional employees to increase sales, there is a cost attached. It is important to understand the numbers associated with running a business. These numbers form the "financial foundation" of a business. A company's spending should not be haphazard, but rather should be the result of careful financial planning. To run a profitable business, you must produce *financial forecasts*. Though personal training businesses may vary, Figure 10 lists some of the sources of income and expenses for this industry.

Income

Personal training sessions	Fitness evaluations
Merchandise (T-shirts, stickers, etc.)	Published materials
Speaking engagements	

Expenses

Rent	Insurance
Advertising	Automobile
Office supplies	Company uniform
Utilities (if applicable)	Computer
Pager/Phone	Printing/Reproduction
Supplies	Accounting
Legal fees	Taxes
Travel	Entertainment
Equipment purchase (if applicable)	

[*Note:* Many personal trainers earn additional income by selling nutritional supplements. This is outside a personal trainer's scope of practice as defined in the American Council on Exercise's Code of Ethics.]

Figure 10

A business plan estimates income and expense by category to establish working income and a cash flow budget. Remember to determine your expense category percentages of total revenue based on the predetermined cost assumptions for total expenses (Figure 11). Too high a percentage in a particular expense group could prove disastrous. Examples of typical percentages of expenses, based on projected or assumed income include:

Expense Percentages of Total Revenue

Payroll ≤ 35%

Rent ≤ 25%

Entertainment ≤ 5%

Accounting ≤ 1%

Figure 11

When starting out, you may want to take on the responsibility of bookkeeping and accounting yourself. This has two advantages: 1) You can keep bookkeeping and accounting expenses to a minimum, and 2) You will learn invaluable information about your company's fiscal health—becoming more attuned and involved in your company's success. If, at a later date, these responsibilities are turned over to a bookkeeper or accountant, you will already have a working knowledge of your company's fiscal health. Before delegating any responsibility, have a firm understanding of how a particular department operates so you can evaluate the work of another paid professional (accountant/bookkeeper). Figure 12 lists some of the types of financial forms with which you should have some degree of proficiency. Figure 13 lists some common financial ratios to help a business owner determine how his or her business is operating and whether or not it is a profitable, solid, and viable operation.

Financial Forms

Income Statement
Shows whether a company is making a profit

Cash-Flow Projection
Details whether a company has the cash to pay its bills

Balance Sheet
Details the overall *net worth* of a company

Figure 12

Financial Ratios

Current Ratio—Current assets divided by current liabilities. This ratio represents a company's ability to finance its current operation and pay off its current liabilities with money to spare.

Quick Ratio—Current assets, minus inventories and prepaid expenses, divided by current liabilities. This ratio represents the ability of a business to meet its current financial obligations, especially its ability to convert its assets into cash quickly.

Debt to Equity—Total Debt divided by Total Equity. This ratio represents how much of a business is owed to all creditors versus equity in the business.

Break-Even Analysis— The point at which there is no profit and no loss. This ratio represents the amount of revenue that must be generated before a profit can begin to be achieved.

Figure 13

Hiring a Bookkeeper and Accountant

"Beware of that which you don't understand."

While hiring a bookkeeper can certainly be beneficial to a business, you can save money by investing in accounting or bookkeeping software. There are a number of programs (e.g., Quick Books Pro™) that help businesses track income, expenses, inventory, payroll, etc. The amount of time and knowledge required to operate these programs is minimal, even for those with limited computer skills. Becoming proficient at these programs allows you to remain firmly rooted in the fiscal health of your company and more attentive to its financial concerns. You can keep your hand on the pulse of the company and chart the financial health of the company with a few clicks of a mouse.

Record Keeping

Hiring a bookkeeper or accountant is relatively simple. However, being able to provide the financial documents these professionals need can become tedious if you do not have a good record-keeping system. Keeping track of a company's expenses and income can become a recurring headache if basic financial bookkeeping rules are not followed. Failing to become competent at record keeping may cause you to lose sight of the company's fiscal responsibilities. There are a number of excellent bookkeeping programs that can assist you as you learn.

As mentioned earlier in this chapter, a working knowledge of business practices is vital to the success of your business. You can assign various responsibilities to outside vendors (accountants, lawyers, advertising representatives, etc.), but should not do so until you have a working understanding of each vendor's function in the company.

Balance Sheet

A balance sheet represents how much a company owns versus how much it owes. It gives a snapshot of the overall financial health of a company: What its value is versus its financial obligations. What a company owns is usually described as a company's *assets*. What a company owes are its *liabilities*. A balance sheet contains such things as a company's current assets, cash, accounts receivable, fixed assets, current liabilities, bank loans, accounts payable, fixed liabilities, and net worth. Figure 14 gives brief descriptions of each and helps define their importance.

Accounting Terminology	
Current assets	Assets a company has that can readily be turned into cash (e.g., bank deposits, inventory, and accounts receivable)
Cash	Money that is immediately available (e.g., currency, checks, and bank deposits)
Accounts Receivable	Money owed to a company by its clients or customers
Fixed Assets	Permanent equipment used in a company
Current Liabilities	Liabilities to be paid within the near future (next 12 months)
Bank Loan	Long-term liability to a banking institution
Accounts Payable	Money the company owes (to vendors, expense accounts, etc.)
Fixed Liabilities	Long-term debt (usually greater than 12 months)
Net Worth	Value of a company after deducting liabilities from assets
Net Income	The difference between a company's total revenue and its total expenses
Gross Income	A company's total revenues, exclusive of any expenses

Figure 14

Income Statements

Income statements, also known as profit and loss statements (P&L) and income and expense statements, detail how profitable a business is after all its revenues and expenses are accounted for. However, an income statement *does not* give a detailed report of how much a company is worth. A company can lose money every month but still have a positive net worth if it owns valuable assets. Additionally, a company can make money each month but have difficulty paying its vendors due to cash-flow problems. Therefore, while a P&L statement details sales (income) and deductions (expenses), it alone does not guarantee the financial health of a company.

Cash-Flow Projections

A company's cash-flow analysis details the amount of company cash. This report is useful in determining whether you can pay vendors, employees, and other expenses. Failure to keep enough liquid cash on hand can jeopardize the future of a business. To most business owners, the monthly cash-flow analysis report is the most important financial assessment because it gives you a clear picture of how much money is coming into and going out of the business. By maintaining accurate records, you are able to plan for future cash management needs using data from prior months or years. Cash-flow analysis is especially important for seasonal or cyclical business owners. Armed with this knowledge, you can better plan expenses and anticipate increases or decreases in cash flow.

> "Cash flow is king. A cash flow analysis is the most important exercise a start-up can do. Do month-to-month cash flow projections. Be conservative. Allow for the things that will inevitably go wrong."
> — *Nancy Glaser, President, Golden Gate Chips*

Below are some tips you can incorporate into your personal training business to maintain control of cash flow:

1. *Budgeting is essential.* A business owner should know a company's monthly expenses rather than "guesstimating" the expenses. Know your company's bottom line.
2. *Collect personal training fees in advance.* This helps eliminate outstanding balances (accounts receivable), which may inhibit monthly cash flow. Avoid the temptation to spend this money in advance!
3. *Get clients to commit to longer-term programs.* Session-to-session payments limit a business owner in projecting revenue for upcoming months. This, in turn, affects a company's budgeting plan.

4. When buying high-priced items for the company, make sure to *negotiate* the longest payment term with the lowest interest rate. Or get the highest discount possible for the purchase price.

5. *Personal training is a seasonal business.* Prepare a budget that allows for fluctuations in revenue.

6. *Be proficient at collecting accounts receivable* if personal training services are not paid for in full. Hiring a billing company is a proficient and cost effective way to collect accounts receivable. For a small fee (a percentage of the company's total monthly revenue) a billing company will debit a client's account and deposit the amount due to the company via electronic funds transfer.

7. Prepare a *contingency plan* for any unforeseen shortages of cash. Alternative lines of credit and other sources of cash should be planned for well in advance.

8. *Update cash flow projections quarterly.* Using historical data allows a company to better appreciate the varying sources of income and expenses.

Measuring Profitability

Entrepreneurs wear many hats while performing a number of duties in their businesses. These responsibilities can range from being a trainer, a manager, and/or an accountant. Having a sound understanding of the financial aspects of a company's operation will enable you to make fact-based decisions and justify future spending for your business.

A basic understanding of accounting principles will assist you in evaluating the future profitability of a prospective service or program. After performing an accounting analysis on a prospective service or program, you are better able to determine whether the program can become a future profit center.

Example: Boot Camp Program Analysis

One program that is very popular with clients is a military-style, fitness boot camp. First determine if there is a demand for such a program. After assessing market potential, the ideal price per class for both the clients' satisfaction and company's profitability. Using the break-even analysis, identify the best price to charge and the time frame in which the program will reach profitability.

First, determine the projected net income of a prospective program for one year (Figure 15).

Once you have projected first-year net income, calculate a prospective program's break-even point (Figure 16a). This analysis will determine whether capital expenses for a new program are justified.

Boot Camp Income Statement

Sales Revenue $14,400
    (144 classes/year x $10 x 10 participants)

Operating Expenses

Manager's Salary $2,000
    (Based on paying owner $50/hour for 40 hours.
    Salary and number of hours are variable based on
    time spent preparing start of each new boot camp)

Instructor's Salary $6,480
    ($45/class x 12 classes/month x 12 months)

Payroll Taxes $ 778
    (varies state-to-state; can be as high as 19%)

Marketing Costs $ 350
    (posters, flyers, etc.)

Maintenance Fees $ 600
    ($50/month x 12 months)

Total Operating Expenses **$10,208**

Net Income **$4,192**

Figure 15

Break-Even Analysis

Fixed Costs $2,000
    (Manager's salary, no equipment expense)

Price per Class $100
    ($10 x 10 clients)

Variable Costs per Class $ 57
    (Total of $8,207.60 operating costs ÷ 144 classes/year)

Break-Even Analysis Equation:

Fixed Costs ÷ (Price per Class–Variable Cost per Class) = Break-even

$2,000 ÷ ($100 - $57) = Break-even

$2,000 ÷ 43 = Break-even

47 ÷ Break-even

47 ÷ 12 (months) = 3.9

Figure 16a

In this example, the annual boot camp break-even point is 3.9 months, based on 12 classes per month.

A more realistic example would have the break-even analysis include the variable of net income since a business owner wants not only to break even, but also to derive an income from a future program. Using the same formulas from above, insert $4,192.40 into the equation (Figure 16b).

Break-Even Meeting Projected First-Year Income

(Fixed Costs +Net Income) ÷ (Price per Class – Variable Cost per Class) = Break-even

($4,000 + $4,192.40) ÷ ($100 - $57) = Break-even

$8,192.40 ÷ 43 = Break-even

190 = Break-even

190 ÷ 12 months = 15 months

Figure 16b

To break even and meet the first year's projected income, the boot camp will require 190 classes or 15 months, based on 12 classes per month.

The final analysis required is the number of clients each boot camp must have to break even (Figure 16c).

Number of Participants Required to Break Even

Total Operating Expenses ÷ Number of Classes = Cost per Class

$10,207.60 ÷ 144 = Cost per Class

$70.89 = Cost per Class

Cost per Class ÷ Income per Member = Break-Even Number of Class Participants

$70.89 ÷ $10 = 7.89

Figure 16c

Therefore each class needs eight clients to break even. Evaluate this number carefully. Although eight clients per class is realistic, the amount of time required to meet the first year's projected income (15 months) is high considering the fixed costs ($2000) are low. The fixed costs are low because there is not any equipment or training expenses. As such, you should expect a low-cost program, such as the boot camp, to break even sooner than 15 months.

Looking at this boot camp model, you can make a profit by reducing the amount paid to boot camp instructors and attracting more clients and classes.

Payment Programs

Clients can pay personal trainers in a number of ways. For any business, advance payments are ideal. This eliminates any *accounts receivable* and the time it takes to collect payment on sessions that *have already taken place!* Beware of pitfalls related to advance payment for services. One common mistake is accounting for the lump sum of money into a current month's revenue and then spending it to pay bills, salary, etc. This revenue should not be "actualized" until the services have taken place. The best place for this money is in a bank earning interest. So whether your company has one employee or many, it should not pay any expenses with revenue that has not been earned (actualized).

Hiring a Billing Company

Given a choice, most business owners would prefer to receive advance payments. However, as mentioned in the previous section, this can create problems with monthly cash flow. An attractive option is to obligate clients contractually to a specific number of months of training and then bill them on a monthly basis. The additional benefit here is that the revenue is still guaranteed (per a signed personal training agreement) and the payments will be made on a monthly basis, thereby assuring the company a specific amount of cash flow each month. As mentioned previously, accepting payment on a session-to-session basis makes cash-flow analysis and projections quite difficult. Having clients pay in full for training sessions (while ensuring prompt payment) can also lead a company to overspend. Receiving monthly payments ensures a company a guaranteed monthly revenue for "X" number of upcoming months.

The key to success for such an approach is to have a payment plan that enables clients to pay month-to-month, while also contractually obligating them to the full amount. Hiring a billing company allows a personal training business to accept Electronic Funds Transfer (EFT) payments. The billing company extracts clients' monthly fees from their respective bank accounts. This guarantees prompt monthly payment. The fee for such services is minimal and is usually a set percentage of a company's monthly billing. A billing company can also, for a small fee, track a company's total clientele so that all pertinent billing and revenue tracking information is accounted for on one monthly report.

Hiring a Payroll Company

"Nothing can be said to be certain except death and taxes."

— Benjamin Franklin

Another responsibility of a business owner is the preparation of payroll. While some business owners have an excellent knowledge of payroll procedures and taxes, hiring a payroll service frees up owners' time to do what they do best: personal training.

While large companies such as IBM and Coca-Cola are not affected by small fluctuations in revenue, the success of a small business is more affected by such changes. Keep in mind: *Preparing your own payroll can be risky!* Why? Paying incorrect payroll taxes can lead to *severe* penalties. Hiring a payroll company can be a lot cheaper than hiring an accountant because accountants usually get paid by the hour. They should be hired for their core services: payroll preparation. This ensures that payroll taxes for each pay period, each quarter, and each year are deducted properly. At the end of the fiscal year, a business owner can present this payroll information (along with other pertinent data on the company's revenue and expenses) to an accountant to prepare the year-end statements. Payroll companies also offer many other additional services such as retirement plans, 401Ks, IRAs, etc.

Legal Stuff

6

Negligence
Failure to exercise the standard of care that a
reasonable person would exercise in like circumstances.

Tort
A private wrong against a person or his/her property.
Aside from certain limited circumstances, all torts arise from
either an intentional, wrongful, or negligent action.

—Business Law, *by J.W. Hardwick and R.W. Emerson*

Chapter at a Glance

Liability Insurance

Negligence and Standard of Care

Other Areas of Concern

Final Thought

This chapter is full of legal terms and should be read carefully. Personal training is a service-oriented business and, as such, results in person-to-person contact on a daily basis. Personal training also places the clients of the business in potentially injurious physical situations. As a trainer, you encourage a client to perform physically demanding work. Therefore, you must not only be qualified to prescribe an individualized workout for each client, but must also know how to handle potentially serious medical situations.

Resistance and cardiovascular training are physically stressful modalities. They are beneficial, if applied correctly, because the body responds to stress and develops stronger muscles, heart, and lungs. If an individual, or a trainer, fails to respect the stress that resistance and cardiovascular training cause, there is the potential for physical injury. Injured clients could sue, so the issue of liability is indeed very important.

Liability Insurance

Be advised: *Do not train a single client before you get liability insurance!* If a client gets injured and can prove that you were negligent, then you may be liable to the injured party. Without insurance, you could end up paying an injury claim out of your own pocket for many years.

Obtaining liability insurance is not difficult. Many of the national personal training associations have a department that deals with insuring personal trainers. If they do not, ask if they contract out such services. For example, the American Council on Exercise offers professional liability insurance to their certified professionals through Fitness Pak. While the cost varies depending upon the coverage being sought (number of employees, size of location, etc.), annual liability should not exceed a few hundred dollars per trainer.

Of Note:

Another reason for an independent trainer to obtain liability insurance is to be able to train clients at existing health clubs. If a health club allows an independent contractor (non-employee) to train on their premises, they will not do so without a contractor's proper insurance documentation. If a health club does allow contractors on their premises, be sure that their club name is listed as an insured party on the insurance policy. Some insurance companies may charge a small fee to add names to an existing policy, but such a fee is a good investment.

Negligence and Standard of Care

Before training your clients, have them sign a Release of Liability form (Appendix H). This form, along with a Personal Training Agreement (Appendix

D), helps protect you in the event that a client takes legal action. Seek out sample industry forms (such as those in the Appendices of this book) or hire a lawyer familiar with contract law to develop company contracts.

These documents are important because personal trainers are required by law to deliver their services in accordance with a *standard of care.* This standard of care may vary from industry to industry but *all* service providers are required by law to provide a standard of care.

Deviations from industry standards of care expose trainers to personal injury claims or lawsuits due to negligence. Negligence can be defined as the failure to exercise the standard of care that a reasonable person would exercise in similar circumstances. If you adhere to the standards of care of a particular certifying agency, you will then have a stronger defense against personal injury claims. It is important to become familiar with and adhere to specific industry guidelines such as exercise testing, lists of coronary risk factors, medical history, contraindications to exercise, etc.

Trainers who are not certified, have no education, or have only a cursory knowledge of standard of care guidelines expose themselves to liability lawsuits. Therefore it is a good idea to start training clients only after 1) earning a certification from a national certification agency, and 2) acquiring liability insurance.

Other Areas of Concern

Some procedures are universal and not subject to the philosophy set forth by one agency. For example:

Health Screening

Personal trainers have a professional obligation to ascertain whether or not a prospective client is fit to exercise. All of the associations mentioned in this book have detailed health-screening processes. It is important to thoroughly screen a client to document this information. Failure to screen a client may subject you to liability issues if the client becomes injured, or other health complications arise.

A popular health-screening tool is the Health History Questionnaire (Appendix E). This questionnaire will help determine whether a client should check with his or her doctor prior to starting an exercise program. By providing this care, a personal training company is adhering to standards promoted within the personal training industry.

Informed Consent

A client's informed consent is important because exercise prescriptions and testing are physically demanding and may result in injury or even death.

By presenting clients with Informed Consent forms (Appendix H), you are informing them of the potential risks associated with said activities. Legally, you are obligated to disclose the risks associated with exercise and exercise testing. By signing an Informed Consent, a client is said to have legally assumed the risks associated with physical training. Should a claim or suit arise later, proof of such consent can help establish the client's knowledge of the risks associated with such activity.

Frequency, Intensity, Time (F.I.T.)

Even after you obtain a signed Informed Consent and decide, via the health screening process, that it is safe for the client to exercise, your professional duties do not end. The recommendations you make should be based on professional standards of activity, and carried out within the parameters of applicable standards of practice. Trainers prescribing exercise programs based on their own personal exercise routines or observation should be warned that such practice is unethical and could qualify as malpractice if a client becomes injured.

Final Thought

The necessity to follow standards of practice requires knowledge of those standards. Failure to have a basic understanding of exercise principles and recommendations increases the chances that a client will become injured. Without the proper education and credentials, you increase your liability. Become certified, obtain insurance, and conduct business policies and practices in a professional and ethical manner!

References

American College of Sports Medicine (2000). *ACSM's Guidelines for Exercise Testing and Prescription.* Philadelphia. Williams and Wilkins.

Hardwick, J.W. and Emerson, R.W. (1992). *Business Law.* New York. Barron's Business Review Series.

## 7

Managing Your Business

"Organize and execute around priorities."
—*The 7 Habits of Highly Effective People,*
by Stephen R. Covey

Chapter at a Glance

Defining Your Company's Purpose

Time Management

Staff Management

Continuing Education / Internships

Deciding on a Payroll Structure

Company Policy and Procedure

Defining Your Company's Purpose

The preceding chapters reviewed the steps necessary to start a business. Now it is time to address the issue of managing that business.

Once a company is legally established it must have policies, guidelines, and a structure in order to run smoothly. Daily, weekly, monthly, quarterly, and yearly, you are faced with tasks that must be completed for the financial and operational well being of the company. You must not only possess knowledge and skills in the health and fitness field. You must also have basic business skills as well. Herein lies the irony. As your business grows, the amount of personal training hours you perform will decrease. More of your "working" hours will be spent dealing with the topics addressed in this and subsequent chapters. A working knowledge of financial, accounting, and business subjects is invaluable.

NOTE: Be prepared to wear many hats when running a business: personal trainer, marketer, accountant, and employer to name just a few.

Time Management

"Whatever humans have learned had to be learned as a consequence only of trial and error experience. Humans have learned only through mistakes." *—Buckminster Fuller*

A personal trainer is not limited to working one-on-one with clients. Unfortunately, too many hours that could be spent productively are often wasted. Let's look at how you can work smarter rather than harder.

Tempus fugit (Latin) = Time flies

The beginning of each day can often be wasted if you wait until the very last minute to plan the training schedule for that day. Inefficiency leads to huge losses of productive time. The best time to plan for a business day is the previous night. Prior to leaving work each night, review the appointments scheduled for the next day, the clients that need to be called, and the location of the appointments. Advanced planning results in proactive, rather than reactive, behavior during the workday. Proactive behavior also helps to produce desired results: business expansion, improved profits, and customer satisfaction.

By prioritizing specific tasks, and acting on those that are important, you can increase their chances of business success. Effective management of one's time requires a knowledge of those tasks or projects that are truly important, versus those that can either be delegated or put on hold.

Also, by setting aside some quiet time at the end of each workday, you become more apt to follow other guidelines that will help improve your professional organization and time-management skills (Figure 17).

Time-Management Guidelines

1. **Plan ahead for the upcoming workday**. Make sure that the next day's appointments are accounted for and a list of people to call has been organized. Be prepared.

2. **Delegate responsibility**. Do not try to do everything yourself. The truth is that delegation greatly increases the time you can spend expanding his business. If scheduling will not accommodate more clients, add one or two new trainers to help free up some time. This could help you earn additional revenue, while providing the time you need to expand the business.

3. **Schedule home-trained clients according to their locale and potential time restraints**. Some trainers maintain a thriving business by performing in-house sessions. Trainers should train clients in particular geographic regions on particular days. This will decrease driving between clients' homes.

   (P.S.: Always **overestimate** how long it will take to get to a client's home!)

4. **Create an efficient filing system**. Disorganization will increase the amount of time it takes to complete a task. Besides being frustrating, such behavior leads to wasted time. Wasted time is equivalent to wasted money.

5. **Become a fan of technology**. Having a pager, cell phone, e-mail, or business phone line provides clients and vendors easy access to your personal training business. Clients need convenient ways to contact you because appointments may need to be changed or canceled for a variety of reasons. Being readily accessible to clients and vendors also increases a company's professionalism. Be prepared for this!

6. **Allocate specific times of the day to make and return phone calls**. Personal training is a business that requires undivided attention. You cannot perform more than one task at a time. This means that business responsibilities must be taken care of when you are not training clients. Remember, even though a personal trainer's day can start at 5 A.M. and end at 10 P.M., most individuals are at work between 9 A.M. and 5 P.M. Therefore, it is extremely important to set aside time during the work day to make and return phone calls.

   P.S. Return phone calls within 24 hours, even if this responsibility must be delegated. This promptness is common courtesy and exudes professionalism.

Figure 17

"Things which matter most must never be at the mercy of things which matter least."   — *Goethe*

Staff Management

"Don't find fault, find a remedy."   — *Henry Ford*

The number of hours a personal trainer can work in a given day is fixed. There is a ceiling on/how much one trainer can earn per day. If you have other trainers working with clients, income grows. However, before hiring additional trainers you should address two concerns:

1. Are you content being a "one-person" operation?
2. If the answer to question number 1 is "no," then be ready to manage the issues associated with a staff (hiring, training, paperwork, communicating, and delegating).

Hiring Trainers

Hiring qualified and competent trainers is not easy. Personal training is a very competitive field. Therefore, the salary paid to a trainer must be competitive. The amount you can pay trainers depends on a variety of factors. The most important one is the company's budget. This raises an important business practice: Prepare financial analyses on a regular basis to better understand the expenses of a business and how those expenses can be minimized or eliminated. Trainers' pay is not an item you can skimp on. An applicant can always go elsewhere with his or her talent. This is not to say, however, that all trainers are worth their asking price. An individual's qualifications, as well as the economic laws of supply and demand, are critical factors to consider.

"Be professional—but, more importantly, be personable."
                                 — *Selling the Invisible*, by Harry Beckwith

Personal training is just that: personal. For a trainer to be an asset to your company, he or she must not only be knowledgeable (certified or have a degree in a related field) but must also possess interpersonal and communication abilities. A trainer must not only be able to foster a professional relationship with his or her clientele, but also must adjust to different demeanors and be able to handle conflicts professionally. The number of certifications a trainer possesses makes no difference if a trainer is unable to inspire, elate, and motivate clientele. It is extremely important to choose trainers who possess good personalities and social skills. Knowledge gaps in other areas can generally be filled.

The Interview Process

For some personal trainers, hiring other trainers to work for them is uncomfortable. For others, the hiring process is pleasurable and signifies company growth. This growth can be hindered, however, if you fail to hire qualified and competent trainers.

The interview process should address three areas of concern.

1. Does the candidate have the skills or experience necessary to perform the duties of a personal trainer?
2. Does the candidate really want the job?
3. Will the candidate "fit in" as a personal trainer?

A thorough interview process cannot be overemphasized. The questions asked should address each of the three aforementioned areas of concern. These questions can be explored further to help you learn more about the candidate in multiple areas (skills, motivation, personality, etc.). Examples of categories and sample questions are listed in Figure 18.

Sample Interview Questions

Getting to Know the Candidate
1. What kind of work do you want to do?
2. How would your friends describe you in terms of character and personality?
3. What are your expectations in the health and fitness field?
4. What goals have you set for yourself professionally? How are you planning to achieve them?
5. Why would you like to work for my company?
6. Tell me about yourself using only one-word adjectives.

Candidate's Work History
1. Tell me about your last job.
2. What did (or do) you enjoy least about your last (or present) job?
3. What's the most important thing you learned from your previous experience that's relevant to this job?
4. Why did you leave your last job?
5. Why do you think you were successful in your last job?
6. Tell me about a method that you've developed to accomplish a task? What are its strengths and weaknesses?
7. What are the most difficult aspects of your current (or former) job, and how do (or did) you approach them?
8. What are some of the basic factors that motivate you in your work?

(continued)

Figure 18

9. What are your long-range goals?
10. What are your leadership skills? Please provide an example that demonstrates them.
11. What were the biggest decisions you made in the past six months?
12. How did you go about making these decisions and what alternatives did you consider?
13. What qualifications do you have to ensure your success in this field?
14. How would you motivate clients?
15. How do you know you are doing a good job?
16. Give an example of a situation in which you failed, and how you handled it.
17. What results did you attain in your last job to cut costs, increase profits, improve morale, and increase output?
18. What was the most useful criticism you ever received?

Determining a Candidate's Motivation

1. What motivates you to put forth your best effort?
2. What can you do, in your position as a personal trainer, when things are slow at work?
3. Why do you think you'll be successful in this job?
4. How do you like to be managed?
5. What's more important to you: salary or a challenge?
6. How important is it for you to learn new skills?

Teamwork Questions

1. Define cooperation.
2. What kind of people do you prefer to work with? Who do you find it difficult to work with?
3. Do you prefer working with others or working alone?
4. Are you a team player?

Can They "Take the Heat"?

1. Tell me about a time when a supervisor (or employer) was not happy with your job performance.
2. Is honesty always the best policy?

Figure 18, *continued*

3. Where do you think the power comes from in an organization?
4. On what occasions are you tempted to lie?
5. Is the customer *always* right?

Can the Candidate Think on His Feet?

1. What's the most significant compliment anyone has ever paid you?
2. Who has been a major influence in your life?
3. How have you benefited from your disappointments?
4. What's the difference between a manager and a leader?

How Important is Money to the Candidate?

1. What do you think you're worth?
2. What value can you add to our company?
3. How do you think compensation should be determined?
4. How can we best reward you?
5. Have you ever worked on commission? Please explain the circumstances.
6. What salary are you asking for?

Assessing Skills

1. Tell me how you are receiving ongoing training and continuing education.
2. Please comment on your technical assessment skills and discuss your strengths and weaknesses.
3. What did you learn from your work experiences or internships?
4. Why did you decide to go (or not) to college?
5. What courses did you like the most/least?
6. What have you done to stay current as a personal trainer in the fitness field?
7. Which of your skills need improvement at this time?
8. Are you a self-starter? Can you give me an example?
9. How would you convince me of the benefits of hiring a personal trainer?
10. How do you try (or would you try) to show each customer that he's important?
11. What's your definition of customer service?
12. Describe a situation in which you went the "extra mile" for a client/customer?
13. If you had a client who complained about poor service, how would you handle it?

Figure 18, *continued*

Continuing Education/Internships

Personal trainers must make sure their education and professional skills remain current. Encourage your staff to pursue a variety of avenues of continuing education. Some of the more common are:

- Obtaining additional certifications such as group fitness instructor or advanced personal trainer, such as ACE's Clinical Exercise Specialist
- Getting published
- Giving a speech or seminar on a health and fitness topic
- Attending industry seminars and conventions
- Obtaining specialty certifications
- Taking courses/Attending workshops
- Reading manuals/books

Each of these examples is an educational experience designed to broaden one's base of knowledge. With so many individuals trying to become personal trainers, it only makes sense to become more knowledgeable and experienced than the competition.

Getting an Advanced or Complementary Certification

To be successful in the fitness industry, you must grow and change, developing a number of competencies along the way. By attaining new skills and knowledge, you enable yourself to provide additional services and reach a more varied clientele. For example, as a certified personal trainer, you can pursue an advanced personal training certification such as ACE's Clinical Exercise Specialist or a complementary certification such as ACE's Group Fitness Instructor. Each of these certifications allows you to provide services to your clients that previously would have been outside your scope of practice.

Distance yourself from the competition—
pursue advanced certifications!

Getting Published

Many personal trainers believe that getting published is difficult. To become published, you need to accomplish two goals: 1) write a health- and fitness-related article, and 2) contact as many editors of magazines and newspapers as possible. It is that simple. The only difficult part is finding the extra time to do this. Once you have written an article, chances are reasonably good that it will be published. While you may not be published in a major health and fitness magazine, you can be assured that there is bound to be at least one publication out there that will accept a relevant and timely article.

Being published is another credential you can add to your resume, which could potentially enable you to charge higher training fees. Remember, fees are based on experience, knowledge, and what the market will bear. If your experiences are professionally broadening, you can justify charging higher rates for your services.

Giving a Speech or Seminar

Giving speeches or seminars is an excellent way to market your personal training company. Fear may prevent more trainers from taking advantage of such great sales opportunities. Many people are apprehensive about speaking to a group of people. Although the personal training venue requires a trainer to be constantly "on-stage," a one-on-one setting with a client is generally more comfortable than public speaking for most people. One should make an attempt to acquire good public speaking skills. Figure 19 presents some target groups for seminars and speeches.

Target Groups for Seminars/Speeches

- Local Chamber of Commerce
- Professional Women's Groups
- Corporations
- Local Schools
- Professional Men's Clubs
- Local Retail Stores
- Local Events

Figure 19

Attend Seminars and Industry Conventions

Seminars and conventions provide great opportunities for trainers to interact and network with others in their profession. You can learn the newest trends, exchange views and ideas, and recruit trainers for available positions within your company. Seminars and conventions are also an easy way to obtain continuing education credits. However, there is one drawback: *cost*. Unless the seminar or convention is local, there may be a substantial cost associated with attending. Assess the benefit attained by attending the event versus its cost. If the benefits outweigh the cost, then go. Remember to choose carefully, because some are better than others.

Deciding on a Payroll Structure

Hiring the Right Trainer for the Job

Ideally, every employee will work as hard as the owner and be just as professional. The reality is that many employees and contractors are driven as much by financial motive as they are by their dedication to health and fitness. While people who become personal trainers *must* be dedicated to their jobs, their desired compensation should be flexible enough to incorporate their own learning curve. Any novice who expects to be paid a relatively high amount should not be hired. Good trainers are individuals who have good interpersonal and communication skills. The knowledge necessary to become a trainer can be acquired; good interpersonal and communication skills cannot. When hiring trainers for your business, place equal emphasis on interpersonal skill and overall knowledge. Selling is about building relationships. Trainers who are unable to build lasting relationships with their clients will not be a successful trainer, thereby hindering your company's future growth.

Devising a Salary Structure

Personal training salaries vary from market to market. There are two criteria you should use in developing a salary structure: 1) How much does the competition pay its trainers? and 2) How much can you afford to pay your trainers? While you should not pay trainers more than the company can afford, you need to recognize whether your proposed fee structure is competitive or not. Devising a competitive salary structure is important to attract competent, long-term employees.

Another issue you will face is the work ethic of each employee. Hire trainers who are hard-working and who maintain high moral standards. The reality is that not every employee is going to be driven to excel at the job. If you pay all employees a flat hourly rate, each employee would be receiving similar compensation. A better salary structure has additional incentives related to employees' performance. For instance, factor in the number of sessions a trainer conducts per week; the number of weekly fitness consultations held by a personal trainer; and the number of weekly leads a personal trainer generates.

Part-time Versus Full-time Employees

Employers who hire part-time employees can determine pay based on an incentive structure or pay a flat percentage of each training fee. For example, a part-time employee might earn 50% of the total training fees he or she generates.

Also, part-time employees are generally not offered benefits or incentives. If you hire full-time employees, offer them incentives and benefits, if possible. Some of these benefits might include:

- Health care insurance (sometimes partial co-pay)
- Professional liability insurance
- Workmen's compensation insurance
- Reimbursement for seminars, workshops, and continuing education courses

Final Note on Payroll Structure

Regardless of the payment method you choose, try to hire trainers who are motivated to both produce revenue and continually update their education. Reward trainers who are the most productive because they will become your company's backbone. If you do not recompense employees through a competitive pay scale, benefits, or incentives, you risk losing them to the competition.

Company Policy and Procedure

To be productive and efficient, a company must have a written code of conduct. These policies and procedures set forth a company's expectations of its employees. Employees should mirror a company's policies and procedures. Therefore, it is very important that each employee provides the standard of care expected by the company (the employer) and by the client. Appendix I illustrates an example of a corporate Policy and Procedure manual.

References

Albrecht, S. (1994). *Service, Service, Service: A Secret Weapon for Your Growing Business*. Massachusetts. Adams Media Corporation.

Covey, S. (1989). *The 7 Habits of Highly Effective People*. New York. Simon and Schuster.

Suggested Reading

Mira, T.K. (1997). *Speak Smart*. New York. Random House, Inc.

8

Marketing

Marketing is not a department. It is your business."

—*Harry Beckwith*

"Tell them what they get, not what you do."

—*Rhonda M. Abrams*

Chapter at a Glance

The Planning Process

> "I can give you a six-word formula for success: 'Think things through—
> then follow through.'"
>
> — *Edward Rickenbacker*

In her book *The Successful Business Plan: Secrets and Strategies* (1991), Rhonda Abrams notes: "If you can't reach customers, you can't stay in business. It's the most basic business truth." Time and care should be devoted to devising an effective marketing strategy. To be effective, marketing efforts must be derived from a sound and organized marketing plan. This chapter covers basic marketing principles and provides guidelines on how you can implement successful marketing plans to promote the business.

Steven Silbiger, in *The Ten Day M.B.A.*, highlights seven key steps in the development of a marketing strategy. These steps provide you with a realistic view of whether or not you have a viable and profitable product. The issue of profitability is addressed by Mr. Silbiger's discussion of identifying a *market segment*. A market segment has to have sufficient size to accommodate a product or service and justify a marketing effort. If the segment is not appropriate or viable, Mr. Silbiger calls this a "makable" product, not a "marketable" one. He goes on to say that *only* marketable products generate revenue.

The development of a marketing plan is an important step that *must* be taken seriously. Take the time to address the issues illustrated by Mr. Silbiger's seven steps. It will assist you in deciding what type of personal training business to manage. The seven steps of a marketing strategy development are:

1. *Consumer Analysis*
2. *Market Analysis*—Analysis of Your Company versus the Competition
4. *Review of the Distribution Channels*
5. *Development of the Marketing Mix* (Four P's: Product, Price, Place, and Promotion)
6. *What Are the Economics of Your Marketing Plan?*
7. *Revision of Plan* (if necessary)

By addressing all seven steps prior to signing a lease for a fitness studio or an exclusive agreement with a health club, you will have more confidence that your marketing plan is viable and that you should start a personal training business. Within every marketing strategy of a business plan there are questions you need to answer to get a better understanding of the potential profitability of your new personal training business (Figure 20).

Marketing Strategy

I. Consumer Analysis

- Is personal training marketable?
- Who hires personal trainers?
- Who influences a client hiring a personal trainer?
- Who needs this service and why?
- What is personal training's value?
- What kind of purchase is personal training (planned/spontaneous)?
- How does personal training meet a consumer's needs?

II. Market Analysis

- What is the nature of the personal training market? Size, growth, product life cycle, for the next 1, 5, 10 years.
- How does your company compete with quality, price, advertising, service, and location?
- What are the trends in the health and fitness industry?

III. Competitive Analysis

- What are your company's strengths?
- What are your company's weaknesses?
- What is your position in the market? Size, share, reputation?
- What resources (e.g. cash, experience, employees) do you possess?
- What are your objectives and strategies?
- What are the barriers to entering the personal training industry?
- What are your back-up plans?
- What are your company's short-term and long-term goals?

IV. Marketing

- Who are you going to target to sell your services?
- **Product**—How are your services unique? Differentiation, perception, packaging, features?
- **Price**—What is your pricing strategy?
- **Place**—How can you best reach your target market?
- **Promotion**—What is the buying process? How is price targeted to the buying-process goals?

(continued)

Figure 20

- How can you use the media for exposure?
- Client promotions: gift certificates, coupons, etc.
- How does price relate to the market, size, product life cycle, competition, etc.?

V. Economics
- Break-even point
- Fixed costs
- Are goals reasonable and attainable?

Figure 20, *continued*

The Four P's: How to Influence Customers to Buy

There are four key components to a sound marketing plan:

1. *Product*
2. *Price*
3. *Place*
4. *Promotion*

These four points lay the foundation for a sound and targeted marketing plan. Regardless of the longevity or size of your company, develop marketing plans to help foster future growth. In addition, a marketing plan must continually evolve because no growing business remains static. To remain competitive, a company must periodically update and fine-tune its marketing plan. For a smaller company this may be required semi-annually, if not quarterly.

Product

The product each reader of this book will be selling is *personal training.* You must address certain issues to help clarify the exact nature of the services offered. Some of these questions are:

- What type of personal training services are offered?
- How long do the personal training sessions last? Determine how the length of each session relates to the wants, needs, and desires of the target market.
- How will the business promote a professional personal-training atmosphere? What certifications/qualifications will the staff have?

- What makes your company's services unique?

When deciding on the type of personal training services your company is going to offer, find a professional niche. Develop a specialty. Too often, companies try to cater their services to a large target audience. Not only is this time-consuming, it is fiscally irresponsible. Personal trainers cannot cater to every single individual. Recognize this business maxim from the outset, and prepare a plan that targets a specific specialty or target population. Examples of these include:

- Sports-specific training (golfers, tennis players, swimmers)
- Post-rehabilitative and/or medical conditions (arthritic, diabetic, stroke and cardiac arrest clients, hearing impaired, etc.)
- Age-specific populations (teenagers, elderly, etc.)
- Home-based clientele

Entrepreneurs with limited capital should decide on a target market. After preparing a marketing plan, you should tirelessly promote your company within this niche.

OF NOTE

A personal training company does not need to be restricted to one-to-one training. Other revenue-generating ideas include:

- Products and/or services
- Clothing line of active apparel with your company's logo
- Internet or home-based workouts and/or fitness evaluations (completed on-line and sent to client)
- Newsletters

Price

Chapter 5 discussed the importance of tracking both fixed and variable business expenses. While marketing costs are a necessary part of business, you must be aware of how such expenses affect the final pricing you offer to your clientele. To prepare your company's *financial forecast,* determine the costs associated with conducting business, the profit margin (break-even analysis), and the target market.

While an accounting degree is not a necessity, a business owner must know the sources of income and expenses to better prepare a sound business plan. Chapter 5 discusses these costs and describes how you can price the products and services you offer.

Set profit margin targets. After preparing a break-even analysis, you should set the prices of your personal training services in order to achieve the desired profit margin. This profit margin, while flexible in nature, must take two factors into account: 1) the competition's pricing schedules, and 2) what the market will bear.

It is certainly acceptable business practice to price one's services above, below, or even equal to the pricing of a competitor. But first decide what your training services are worth, and then market according to that pricing structure.

Important Note

The most important consideration in determining pricing structure is careful planning. Learn the different costs associated with running a business (see Chapter 5), and the profit margin of your training services. Know the target market. This data must be assembled before you make pricing decisions.

Place

Training clients in an established health club exposes you to a large target population and also helps decrease outside marketing expenses, since most current clientele will be drawn from the health club's existing membership.

Personal training is a service not affordable to everyone. You must recognize the financial limitations of your potential consumers (clients). *Do not select a mass distribution strategy.* Mass distribution strategies are adopted by companies with products affordable to the majority of the population. The exclusive treatment involved in personal training makes it a product targeted to a select population. Carefully scrutinize what your target population (residential or commercial) is, and what type of setting or facility will appeal to such people. Do not forget that one of the most important considerations to take into account is convenience. Consider where the business is to be located and whether or not the surrounding neighborhood(s) can provide a steady stream of clientele able to afford such a service.

20 Low-Cost, High-Impact Marketing, Advertising, and Promotion Ideas

"Advertising works on what is called the Rule of Seven, which asserts that a message typically needs to be noticed by any given customer seven times before he or she will take action. The corollary to the rule is that it takes an average of three tries to get noticed once. That means you have to expose a potential customer to your products an average of twenty-one times before he or she's likely to call, come in, or place an order."

— Getting Business to Come to You, *(1991).*
Edwards, Edwards, and Douglas

Bartering

Bartering has long been used as a way for two individuals, or companies, to benefit from the other's services or products. Take advantage of bartering. The cost to you is your own personal time; there is no outlay of cash (expenditure). Bartering can be performed to gain exposure for a company (new or established), and to provide a product or service at little or no cost.

When making a decision of whether or not to barter, consider which industry or trade group to target. Listed below are examples of bartering that have been used by professional trainers to increase their company's exposure to the general public.

Train a Radio D.J.—Agree to train a radio personality for a period of time (three to six months). In return, he must mention that he is starting an exercise program and has enlisted the free services of your personal training company. Invariably, over the course of the training, the radio personality will mention your company repeatedly on his show.

Train the Owner of a Printing Shop—Being able to barter services with a printer will save you a tremendous amount of money on the costs of brochures, business cards, letterhead, gift certificates, postcards, etc. While the personal training provided might not cover a company's entire printing costs, bartering training in exchange for such services will save money.

Train the Owner of a Health Club—If you do not want to take on the fiscal responsibility that goes with owning your own personal training studio, a good way to make inroads with a local gym is to train its owner or general manager. This approach will work if you have first established that the health club would be receptive to your company's services (acting as an independent contractor). By training the owner, you gain the respect and confidence of an important individual who can refer potential clients to your personal training company.

Train a Lawyer and/or an Accountant—No business should operate without the services of a lawyer and an accountant. A good way to save money is to distribute flyers touting your personal training services to local law and accounting firms. Another approach is to obtain a list of a law or accounting firm employees' names. Then send personalized letters suggesting the formation of a professional alliance for the bartering of desired services (personal training, legal assistance, and accounting).

Remember, some of these ideas may not work for every training company. It is important to note that every new business is going to have limited working capital. As such, it is important to pursue avenues that will help decrease cash expenditures and enhance your marketing and financial position.

Brochures

Brochures provide important information on your company (Figure 21). They should be designed to answer the most commonly asked questions and to raise additional client questions, thus enticing the prospect to call.

Brochure Use

1. Brochures help initiate a relationship with a prospect.
2. Brochures give a company credibility.
3. Brochures help diminish sales tension because they allow a prospect time to study your company's services.
4. Brochures help answer any questions a prospect may have regarding your company's services.

Figure 21

Brochures are best utilized when they are professionally written and presented in an eye-catching layout. They should include graphics, terminology describing your personal training services, testimonials, calls to action, and pertinent company information (name, address, phone numbers). Here are the four steps to developing the content of your brochure:

1. Decide what aspects of your business to emphasize. You cannot include everything, so be selective and targeted.
2. Explain any special services or products that may attract new customers.
3. Keep the brochure simple and professional, keeping in mind it is a reflection of your organization.
4. Do not include fee information. Instead, ask them to call or stop by for more information.

Brochures can be costly, so do not mail them randomly. Send brochures to qualified prospects or a pre-qualified population (e.g., direct mailing lists incorporating the names of individuals living in a particular demographic region and having a certain median income).

Business Cards

Do not let business cards stay in a filing cabinet, on employees' desks, or in wallets. Business cards are miniature billboards that help distinguish your business. A business card *must* include a company's name, address, phone, fax, e-mail, your name, and a positioning statement. A positioning statement describes the services your company provides. While most personal training companies utilize names that allude to health and fitness, a positioning statement helps clarify for a potential client exactly what services a company provides. Examples include: *"Personal fitness training for ALL ages"* or *"The personal training specialists."*

Few people take advantage of the empty space on the back of the card. Use promotions or catch phrases that will persuade prospects to hold onto the business card. If they hold onto the card, chances are they will remember not only the company name, but also the services it provides. Some ideas for the back of the card are *"Call today for a FREE Consultation,"* *"20% off any training package,"* or *"First personal training session is FREE!"*

Camps and Clinics

One-to-one training may be expensive for an individual client. A great way for a company to attract new clients is by offering lower-cost group camps and clinics. Group sessions promote challenging and motivating exercises, with the participants paying a fraction of the cost of One-to-One personal training. However, note that each requires specialized training, skill, and experience to conduct these classes.

Some other ideas include:

- Self-defense clinics
- Prenatal clinics
- Golf Conditioning
- Plus 55 Camps (group classes targeted to older populations)
- Injury clinics (include local specialist)

Clubs

Clubs are able to offer camps and clinics year-round. A personal training company can start Running Clubs, Weight Lifting Clubs, and Health Watch Clubs, to name a few. You can start these clubs on your own or form professional alliances with others to provide these services on a continual basis.

A company can form a running club and have paying participants train for a specific road race (10K, 10 mile, 1/2 marathon, marathon, etc.), or teach participants different ways to run (e.g., steady state, track, fartlek, interval, and hills training).

Determine the fixed costs that will be associated with the program (race fee, instructor fee(s), flyers, banners, etc.), and include a profit margin that is reasonable. Then establish a fee per participant.

Charitable Donations

Presenting charities with donations (monetary, volunteer services, material objects) is a way for a company to build good will in the community. While some business owners may disagree, it is a good business practice. And you will attain recognition for your company from such charitable acts.

Here are some ideas:

1. *Donate company time for a charity road race.* Personal trainers can help runners stretch before and after the race and also dispense water. Depending on the event, you may gain permission to have a booth or stand. Promote your services by wearing your company shirt. Check with race organizers in your area for more information.

2. *Donate time at a local hospital and/or retirement home.* Personal training companies can make contacts for future referrals and earn the respect of the medical community by performing charity work. Doctors can, and will, refer patients to personal trainers they know and trust.

3. *Organize a party for a good cause.* Hosting a party for a charity can help raise money, awareness, and name recognition for your company.

4. *Donate company funds to sponsor an event or team.* Personal training companies can be a sponsor in local health events. You can also sponsor local recreational groups, such as little league teams or youth basketball.

Client Subscriptions

Offering subscriptions to health- and fitness-related journals, newsletters, and magazines is an excellent way for your company to market itself. Many publications, including *ACE FitnessMatters*, offer a bulk rate to personal trainers. *ACE FitnessMatters* is published bimonthly by the American Council on Exercise. For more information, log onto www.acefitness.org.

Company Name and Tagline

One of the first items a prospect encounters when investigating a personal training company is the company name and its tagline. A company name must be representative of the health and fitness industry. While it is not necessary to have the words "personal training" in the business name, the name and the tagline must communicate that the company specializes in personal fitness training. For example, it would not be prudent to start a health and fitness business with the name Joe's Training Center. Individuals might think that Joe's company specializes in classroom training services. Think carefully about your company's name, as people will draw conclusions based on it.

Do not hesitate to design a short, descriptive phrase ("tagline") that adds information or meaning to a business name. Taglines are useful in that they help convey a certain image. Many Fortune 500 companies use taglines with their names.

Coca-Cola— "It's the real thing."

American Express— "Never leave home without it."

Maxwell House Coffee— "Good 'til the last drop."

Co-op Advertising

Co-op advertising is used by retailers and manufacturers to generate additional sales. This is how it works: Computer Store Megaplex advertises in the local papers touting the brands of computers it offers. Prior to placing the advertisement, the computer store negotiates with each computer manufacturer to pay a percentage of the ad cost. The result is that Computer Store Megaplex advertises, while sharing the cost with computer manufacturers.

Co-op advertising is a useful way to enhance a company's presence in a market at a fraction of normal cost. Personal training businesses are not manufacturers or retailers, but this business niche can save money on advertisement costs by "co-opting" the cost with a business in a field that complements this industry (e.g., chiropractor, equipment manufacturing stores, nutritionists, massage therapists). The personal training company gains name and product publicity. Another benefit is that your company can network with these related industries (nutritionists, therapists, etc.) for future clients and other future marketing ideas.

Direct Mail

Direct mail is also a useful way to advertise to your target market. Direct mail costs are relatively inexpensive and allow you to focus your marketing efforts on a specific population.

Figure 22 lists items a business owner should address when conducting direct mailing campaigns.

To target a specialized segment of the population, *rent a mailing list*. Mailing lists are highly specialized to meet the characteristics of typical clientele. Mailing list companies can create lists based on gender, age, occupation, hobbies, income, demographics, nationality, and marriage status, to name a few. Do not underestimate the importance of purchasing a targeted mailing list; the success of your campaign depends on it.

A good place to start is the Standard Rate and Data Service (SRDS) direct mail catalog. This book contains more than 10,000 different mailing lists. After you define a group to target, the SRDS can help carefully select a mailing list that fits your criteria. Of note: The SRDS does not rent lists, so business owners must contact a list broker or mailing list company.

Companies that sell mailing lists generally grant only a one-time usage. If you want to re-mail to the same "population" in the near future, you must purchase another list. Be advised that mailing list companies can track whether a company is sending more than one mailing to each purchased name.

Direct Mailing Campaigns

A *successful* direct mail campaign will attain a hit-rate of 2 or 3%, so be very frugal as you plan, and think about the cost of the entire campaign and how it compares with this rate of return. A good tip is the 40-40-20 rule, which states that 40% of your success depends on your message, 40% on the quality of your mailing list, and 20% on the design of your mailer.

1) The artwork and the copy must be done professionally to maximize effectiveness.

2) The mailing list should be specialized to ensure that mailings are sent to the right prospects.

3) The direct mail should grab the reader's attention. Edwards and Douglas (1991) note that such attention can be obtained by promoting a product or service that's of particular interest to the target market or by designing the direct mailing in a unique way so that the recipient is compelled to look at it more closely. Either way, the authors note, your prospect will read your mailing, which in turn, can create interest.

4) The mailing should contain a call to action and/or propose a limited time offer.

Words that Call for Action

Limited time . . . Call today . . . Join today . . . Exclusive promotion . . . Limited availability . . . Free!

Figure 22

Circulars

Circulars (or flyers) are an inexpensive way to promote your company. The copy must be well written and include an attention grabber to promote a call to action. If you have limited writing skills, hire a professional to write copy and perform desktop publishing, which is relatively inexpensive. The difference between success and failure with a flyer generally boils down to the words chosen and how well it is designed. Circulars must include an attention grabber, company name, address, fax number, e-mail address, office number, and a special offer or promotion.

Distribute circulars within a specific target market and remember to consider the geographic location. Distribute circulars only to the region to which you are catering. When distributing flyers door-to-door, *do not* put circulars in a homeowner's mailbox. It is against the law. It is also against the law to solicit people on certain public property (e.g., malls, shopping centers). So check with property managers or research local ordinances before handing out company circulars.

Free Publicity

Publicity is free advertising. Getting your name, your business, or your services mentioned in the press or on the radio is a great way to reach potential customers that you would not reach through other forms of advertising. Also, publicity generates word of mouth amongst potential customers, enhancing your company's name and visibility.

Press Releases

Sending out press releases is a very useful way to get free publicity. Press releases are short news stories featuring a company and its services. They are mailed to the editors of publications who might be interested in running a story based on its contents. But because editors receive virtually hundreds of press releases per month, the releases must contain a newsworthy story, angle, hook, or other interesting information. To write a powerful and interesting press release, and increase your chances that publications will run them, follow these suggestions:

1. The topic covered in the press release must be *eventful.* While publications may run one-line mentions regarding promotions or changes in corporate locations, most will overlook such "news" for more interesting topics.
2. The topic must be *meaningful* to the publication's readership, not to your personal training company.
3. The press release must contain *incentives* for the reader *to pay attention.* If there is no benefit to the reader, or they do not find a release informative in some way, the press release will not be effective.
4, Include a call to ACTION! Give the reader a reason to call! Offer a free fitness consultation, a free workout, or a free evaluation. Anything to make that phone ring, and have a prospect take that first step.

Appendix J contains an example of a press release designed to grab a reader's attention and inspire readers of all ages to start exercising.

Radio Expert

Being interviewed on a radio show as an expert is a great way to gain free publicity. First, convince radio producers you have knowledge and expertise that can be helpful, insightful, and beneficial to a producer's radio program(s). A radio producer can learn about a personal training company via a professional connection, press release, personal letter, or personal phone call. Do not hesitate to use each avenue of contact and use them frequently. Radio producers are generally very busy people, so a company's press release or phone inquiry may not stir them to respond. That is o.k. Try again, and again, and again. When the topic of personal training is relevant to an upcoming show, your company is the one he or she might remember. It only takes getting on the radio once before you can market yourself as a "fitness expert on the radio."

Gift Certificates

Gift certificates are a must for a business owner. Whether you give them to current clients, offer them to qualified prospects, or use them to gain referrals, gift certificates are a great way to attract new business and keep existing business.

What better way to thank loyal clients than by sending them a gift certificate thanking them for their business? You will reap the rewards of this client's business for months, if not years, to come. Remember: 80% of the revenue of a business comes from current clients, so do everything to let them know they are appreciated.

Gift certificates are also useful marketing tools to offer to a prospective client who has inquired about personal training services. After meeting and speaking with the prospect, send a personalized note thanking him for his or her time, and include a gift certificate that is good for reduced-price training rates or apparel.

Current clients are also a good source of new personal training prospects. Ask your clients if they know of anyone who would benefit from personal training services. If they do, give the client a gift certificate in the new prospect's name, and have them pass it on to the new prospect. Good rapport with clientele ensures that such gift giving will turn into future sales.

Do not cut corners when designing gift certificates. Like business cards, gift certificates must convey a strong message and be of excellent quality. Aside from utilizing the "$$ Off" approach, make up 12 gift certificates corresponding with each month of the year. Each is good for one workout during a particular month. A prospect then has 12 chances to use your services.

Internships

Internships are another way for a trainer to gain valuable exposure, as well as earning the respect of other professional colleagues. Volunteering can be performed in a variety of fields (e.g., a physical therapy clinic, a cardiac clinic, or a corporate wellness center). Most training certifications typically prepare a personal trainer for "*apparently healthy populations*, while others, such as the ACE Clinical Exercise Specialist prepare trainers to work with special populations. Volunteering within such communities can give you exposure, and also promote the confidence of industry professionals in your abilities.

Newsletters

Producing a company newsletter is a good way to convey information that might otherwise be difficult to report to your clients. It is a good way to inform your clients of awards the company has received, or some outstanding facts about personal trainers or clients. A newsletter can also contain fitness anecdotes, recipes, industry news, jokes, and health and fitness information.

Postcards

Rather than send prospects letters in envelopes (which are costly) take the more economical route and mail postcards. Postcards with a preprinted offer are also usually cheaper to produce than a color brochure.

Levinson and Godin, in *The Guerilla Marketing Handbook* (1994), note that color postcards can increase readership by 41% and raise a buyer's inclination to buy by nearly 26%. Raising a buyer's inclination sets the buying process in motion.

Public Speaking

Public speaking can be a useful way to market your business. It is inexpensive (costing only your time), and allows you (the "expert") to address your prospective audience. Unlike a one-dimensional ad that some prospects may read and put aside, public speaking allows you to speak to an audience and convince them of the need to improve the quality of their lives.

Use local clubs and associations to get your company name out there. Speak at women clubs, men's clubs, professional clubs, or associations. Speak to any group that comprises a target population. Remember, as long as a personal training company stays within a reasonable geographic region, most of corporate America can be considered "potential" clients.

Quality Logo

Logos create images. The logo chosen to represent your company will convey messages to its potential market. These messages help potential clients identify your company and the services it offers. Logos therefore help position health and fitness companies within their industry, and project an image of professionalism.

Brand recognition takes years to develop. Incorporate a logo that is professional looking, presents the appropriate image of the business, and is easily remembered and recognized by the target market. *Do not try to save money by producing a poorly drafted logo.* The company logo is one that must stand the test of time, because your company's image is its link to potential markets.

Referrals

A large percentage of new clients in the fitness industry come from referrals. *Do not ever lose sight of this.* All the advertising in the world will not bring in as much new business as comments from satisfied clients. Though it is great for business, merely having happy clients will not help your business grow. You need to ask current clients for referrals. Different methods can be used to achieve this (e.g., postcards, letters, and meetings). Seasonal promotions can also help boost referrals from current clientele. Appendices K and L provide examples of seasonal promotions.

Testimonials

Testimonials promote a business and the quality of its service. A testimonial is a statement from a satisfied client thanking the company for its services. Testimonials can benefit a company's promotional campaign if they are included in brochures, direct mail, advertisements, flyers, or press releases.

Some testimonials are received unsolicited, but usually business owners need to ask satisfied clients to give a testimonial.

By requesting testimonials regularly from its clients, you can continually update your testimonial list and direct its printed materials (including testimonials) to a target market. Figure 28 lists some sample testimonials used in promotional efforts.

Internet Marketing

A Web site is a revolutionary communications tool that offers business owners great reach and opportunity. You can market your services in ways that are limited only by your own imagination. The Internet provides a low-cost, wide-reaching medium that you can use for all types of promotional, research, and revenue generating activities.

Creating a Web Site

To promote your company or sell services and products on the Internet, you must create a Web site. The first step is to register a domain name. Your domain name, or Web site address, should be the same name as your company or describe your company in some way. The Web site address will be something like www.YourCompany.com. You can research Web site domains and purchase your domain name directly from www.networksolutions.com. After you have purchased your domain name, you'll need to find a company to host your Web site. There are several hosting organizations to choose from. You can either do a search on the

Internet or go through the phone book to find one that best suits your needs. ConnectNet and MindSpring are two popular hosts. Most hosts charge a monthly fee that ranges anywhere from $25 to $200, depending on the depth of your site. You can also create a Web site and get hosting or your domain name free of charge in exchange for carrying advertisements on your site. Again, use the Internet to search for organizations that offer free services. ACE also offers an inexpensive Web site solution for ACE-certified fitness professionals. To learn more about it, visit the ACE Pro Site at www.acefitness.org.

Now that you've registered your domain name and are hosting it, you need to design it. When designing a Web site, take a look at competitors' sites. This will provide an overview of how other companies in your market promote their businesses and market their services. You should then write a Web site business plan. Outline your goals and objectives as well as the details on how you plan to reach them. Your next step is to hire a Web designer. You can learn HTML and basic graphic design skills yourself, but hiring a Web designer can save you a lot of time and frustration. Just be sure to hire an individual or organization that offers both programming and graphic design. Be sure to ask for references and view other sites they have created. While you create your site, refer back to your Web site business plan often and be sure the designers understand your business goals as well. Keeping your goals and objectives in mind, create a user-friendly Web site that offers users a value or benefit.

Six Ways to Market Your Web Site

There are millions of Web sites on the Internet competing for visitors. Therefore, it is important to market your Web site effectively. Marketing on the Web allows you to reach an audience you may not otherwise reach, and possibly stay ahead of the competition.

(1) Everything Your Customers See and Hear

Put your company's Web site and your e-mail address on all company letterhead, business cards, brochures, catalogs, advertisements, packaging, answering machines and voice mails, and other marketing materials. You should also create an e-mail signature, which is a listing of information at the bottom of all outgoing e-mail messages. While such signatures can vary in length, it is best to restrict them to your name, the company name, mailing address, phone and fax numbers, e-mail address, Web site address (URL), and a brief sentence explaining the company's services and benefits.

The more ways a company can get their Web site and e-mail address marketed to its target audience, the greater the chance that the company will attract new prospects.

(2) Search Engines

When people surf the Internet, they do not always look for new sites, instead they type key words into a search engine such as Lycos.com or Excite.com. Search engines are large indexes that search the Internet or their database for Web sites that match the entered keyword. Whenever you hit the search button on your browser, you are entering a search engine. All search engines allow you to post your site so it can be found when keywords that fit your company's background are typed into the search engine. Go to all the search engines and submit your Web site. You can usually find the link to submit your Web site on the bottom of their home page.

In addition to using search engines, people also use Web directories such as www.yahoo.com, which function the same way as search engines in that they are opened when you click the Search button on your browser, but the keyword may be in several different directories or categories. For example if you do a search for "personal trainer" you will notice that it will be listed in the "Health >Fitness" category as well as the "Region>Country>USA>City>San Diego" and others like it. When choosing directories it is very important to choose categories carefully. Determining a directory that is appropriate for your Web site will make the difference in the number of people who visit the site.

(3) Content is King

Now that people are coming to your Web site, you need to give them something valuable in order to keep them interested long enough to purchase your services. Offering your customers good content in the form of articles or an electronic newsletter works best. Articles for electronic newsletters can be as short as one page, or even one paragraph. You can write the content yourself or purchase content from syndication companies that manage content for large Web sites. Whatever you do, do not steal content from another Web site or publication, as this is a form of plagiarism. If you want to use content from a Web site, contact them and they may sell you the content or give it to you in exchange for promoting their Web site.

You may also use an electronic newsletter. If you are going to offer an electronic newsletter, you may need to purchase e-mailing or listserve software to facilitate the e-mails, depending on the number of subscribers you have.

Not every e-mail newsletter is free. Some companies charge for their services. While an argument can be made that subscription fees might turn away visitors to your company's site, many sites do make money charging subscription fees.

(4) Guest Book

One of the objectives in your Web business plan will probably be to generate leads. An easy way to get names, mailing addresses, and e-mail addresses of those surfing your Web site is by creating a guest book. If you have an electronic newsletter, you can use it to collect information. If not, offer something valuable in exchange for providing their information (e.g., a drawing to get a discount on personal training services).

Keep in mind that people do not like their personal information sold, so it is a good idea to post a disclaimer on your Web site that lets visitors know how you are going to use the information.

(5) Linking with other Web Sites

An effective means of promoting your company's Web site is by linking it to like-minded sites. Surf the Web, find sites that are complementary, and call these companies to find out if they would like to exchange links.

(6) Response Templates

Once your company has an e-mail address and a Web site, you will receive inquiries regarding your services online. By developing a response template, you can respond to prospective clients while also marketing yourself. A response template is an e-mail that includes key benefits to your company's personal training services, a short description of its services, brief testimonials from satisfied customers, and some kind of offer that prompts prospects to inquire about and buy its services.

Any company that has an e-mail address receives unsolicited e-mails. You can turn these e-mails into potential prospects by replying using the company's response template. Instead of deleting unwanted e-mail information, you are sending out marketing material!

References

Beckworth, H. (1997). *Selling the Invisible: A Field Guide to Modern Marketing*. New York. Warner Books.

Edwards, P., Edwards, S., and Douglas, L.C. (1991). *Getting Business to Come to You*. New York. G.P. Putnam's Sons.

Levinson, J. and Godin, S. (1994). *The Guerilla Marketing Handbook*. New York. Houghton Mifflin Company.

Suggested Reading

Maas, J. (1984). *Better Brochures, Catalogs and Mailing Pieces*. New York. St. Martin's Press.

Levinson, J.C. (1985). *Guerilla Marketing: Secrets for Making Big Profits from Your Small Business*. New York. Houghton Mifflin.

Levinson, J.C. (1989). *Guerilla Marketing Attack*. New York. Houghton Mifflin.

Beemer, C.B. (1997). *Predatory Marketing*. New York. William Morrow and Co.

Sandhusen, R.L. *Marketing*, 2nd ed. New York. Barron's Educational Series, Inc.

9

Networking

"We are not dependent on each other; nor are we
independent of each other; we are all
interdependent with each other."
—*Bob Burg*

"You can get everything in life you want if you just
help enough other people get what they want."
—*Zig Ziglar*

Chapter at a Glance

For most business owners networking is a double-edged sword. On one hand, it opens up avenues of potential future sales. On the other, it's a time-consuming task that's widely underutilized. The painful truth is that most people don't enjoy attending functions in order to meet people they don't know to distribute business cards and maybe make a few contacts. Meeting other professionals and making business contacts is one of the lifelines to any business. Use these functions and opportunities as ways to fine tune social skills and to get to know a variety of people from different professional backgrounds.

Establishing Relationships with Other Health and Fitness Professionals

One of the ways businesses succeed is through their single-minded approach to professionalism. They strive to improve every aspect of their company each and every business day. These companies constantly develop new ways to pursue new business, so that they can stay ahead of their competition. Personal trainers can strengthen their professional image by creating a networking team of other local health and fitness professionals. The importance of networking can't be overstated. Meet others with whom mutually beneficial alliances can be formed.

Figure 23 lists other health professions that may help increase the visibility and professional image of a company.

Networking Health Alliances

- Primary Care Physicians
- Chiropractors
- Massage Therapists
- Physical Therapists
- Orthopedists
- Podiatrists
- Nutritionists
- Health-food Store Owners

Figure 23

Improving Professional Image and Visibility

Personal training as an industry isn't monitored by federal or state regulations—as long as the care given does not extend beyond working with "apparently healthy" people. Other health and fitness professionals are understandably skeptical about trusting a personal trainer to work with one of their clients. To alleviate this concern, personal fitness trainers must demonstrate a certain degree of aptitude before trust on the part of a health care professional can be attained.

Ways to Network

Chamber of Commerce

Joining a local chapter of the Chamber of Commerce exposes a business owner to a myriad of potential business opportunities (e.g., legal counsel, bookkeeper, printer, supplier, etc.). Each time you come into contact with a person, corporate entity, or association, it is imperative that you present yourself in the best light possible. Remember, you don't get a second chance to make a first impression. Go out of your way to determine how each contact can help your company grow.

Community Involvement

Community involvement not only provides opportunities for potential new business but also allows you to give something back to the community. According to Paul and Sarah Edwards and Laura Clampitt Douglas in their book *Getting Business to Come to You* (1991), community involvement provides the following advantages:

1. Increased Visibility
2. Positive Publicity
3. Exposure to Community Officials and Decision Makers
4. Increased Credibility
5. Low Cost

Three ways Edwards, et al. (1991) recommend to become active within a business community are:

1. Volunteering
2. Donations
3. Sponsorships

Start your own Networking Group

A network group doesn't have to be extensive or elaborate. The basic premise behind starting such a group is to bring together professionals from unrelated businesses. This allows you to build a professional referral network with businesses outside the health and fitness industry. This is important because a trainer will have clients who invariably seek information and contacts for many industries (dry cleaning, restaurants, hair salons, sporting goods, lawyers, accountants, etc.). According to Bob Burg, in his book *Endless Referrals* (1994), there are three intentions of a networking group:

1. To develop and maintain give-and-take relationships with other business owners and professionals.
2. To train each of these businesspeople to outline and describe your services, thereby increasing referrals.
3. To try to establish relationships with another group member's "sphere of influence"— the elaborate realm of people each of us can claim as our own network of various professional and personal relationships.

Networking groups must meet on a regular basis, have a formalized meeting agenda, and discuss relevant topics. Most important to the success of a networking group is that every member builds relationships with other businesspeople, week in and week out. Remember, the purpose of a networking group is qualified leads, leads, leads, and more leads!

Train Others to Prospect for your Company

How often do you meet people in a social situation who ask you what you do for a living? These situations can open doors of opportunity for the fitness professional. Always have a two- to three-sentence description that succinctly summarizes personal fitness training (e.g., "Personal Training Business, Inc. helps improve the quality of life of our clients by meeting their personal fitness needs."). And try to educate the person about the type of people who most frequently use personal training services. This serves to plant the seed for future referrals. Subconsciously, such people will think of others in their "sphere of influence" who might benefit from the services of a personal trainer. They'll only refer friends to those they like. So remember always to be kind, courteous, and most of all, make a lasting impression.

Giving Talks and Writing Articles: Make Yourself an Expert

In order to gain professional recognition, a businessperson must establish credibility. The media provides instant credibility to a fitness trainer's prospects and potential networking pool. By addressing specialized groups or writing and publishing a health and fitness article, you can bring yourself into contact with a wide range of people.

The key is follow-up. Send promotional literature to those who have attended talks or seminars. Always remember to "give" first. The return on such an investment will be much higher.

Promoting for Others

Promoting for others is another example of "giving to get." Before expecting an endless stream of referrals from another health professional, a business owner must first extend an opportunity for that other professional to benefit. By offering to provide referrals to a specific health professional (chiropractor, nutritionist, massage therapists, etc.), a business owner builds professional relationships bound by respect. Companies can use coupon mailers in their "New Client Packets" to help promote specific health professionals (see Figure 24). Companies should not initially request reciprocity. Over time, as the health professional receives referrals, he will invariably send referrals in return. Be patient, and get creative.

Networking Tips

"God gave us two ears and one mouth for a reason."

—Ancient proverb

Invariably, business owners will need to attend events where they can promote their businesses (e.g., Chamber of Commerce, women's groups, men's groups, professional groups, etc.). To manage time most effectively, utilize the following networking tips:

1. Bring plenty of business cards. Exchange cards with everyone.
2. Mingle, mingle, mingle. Don't avoid socializing. Start conversations and try to interact.
3. Ask questions about those you meet. The best way to get to know others, and to get them to like you, is to ask them questions about themselves and what they do professionally.
4. Dress appropriately.
5. While networking, do not sell! The purpose of networking is to make contacts, not sell to people (at least not yet).
6. Create a professional contact file, which is continually updated after each networking event. Be sure to write down a brief description of the contacts on the backside of their business cards to help better remember their particular professional responsibilities, authority, personal likes, dislikes, etc.
7. Send follow-up notes to those you've met, possibly including a company brochure and business card.
8. When referring others to a particular business or service, refer them to those in your contact file. Tell the prospect to let the business person know that "Company X recommended I call..."

Networking Etiquette

1. Always say thank you to someone who sends a referral! Think about how you would feel if you sent another professional a referral and they didn't have the courtesy to call or write a note of thanks! These individuals would be removed from your contact file for good.

2. When you refer a prospect to someone on your contact list, make sure it's a good fit. For example: You send one of your clients to a bookkeeper you know professionally but don't know what types of clients the bookkeeper works with or what fees he charges. You'll be setting up either the prospect or the bookkeeper for an embarrassing encounter. Either way, you'll lose credibility.

3. Do what you say you're going to do. If you tell someone in your network that you'll call him within twenty-four hours to discuss future networking ventures, call within the allotted time. Failure to meet commitments will hurt your professional credibility. Since a large majority of new personal training clients come from referrals, sustaining professional credibility is cheaper than trying to attract new clients from paid advertisements!

4. Give, give, give. Don't expect immediate referrals from others. Rather, spend energy figuring out ways you can provide referrals to your contact list. By placing an emphasis on giving first, you build a network of professionals who like you and are indebted to you for some of their business. In time, they'll send referrals to your personal training business. More likely than not, the amount of business they send you will outweigh your initial time spent prospecting for them.

References

Burg, B. (1994). *Endless Referrals*. McGraw-Hill, Inc. New York

Edwards, P., Edwards, S., and Douglas, L.C. (1991). *Getting Business To Come To You*. G.P. Putnam's Sons. New York.

Suggested Readings

Erdman, K., and Sullivan, T., (1992). *Network Your Way to Success*, Philadelphia, Marketers Book Shelf.

Hokins, T. (1988). *How to Master the Art of Selling*, New York, Warner Books.

Lipnack, J. and Stamps, J. (1988). *The Networking Book,* New York, Viking Press.

Mackay, H.B. (1991). *The Harvey Mackay Rolodex Network Builder*, Secaucus, New Jersey, Taylor Publising.

## 10

Customer Service

"There is only one boss: the customer. And he can fire everybody in the company, from the chairman on down, simply by spending his money somewhere else." —*Sam Walton*

"Don't open a shop unless you know how to smile." —*Old Jewish Proverb*

Chapter at a Glance

The Competitive Edge
Rules of Customer Service
Relationship Reinforcers

The Competitive Edge

"Quality service is what our company must provide, through the careful management of our strategies, systems, and people to meet and often exceed the needs and expectations of our current and new external and internal customer. By creating a service-driven organization, we can capture more market share, offer more value than our competitors, and establish a workplace environment that is profitable, healthy, and beneficial to everyone who works with it and for it."

— *Service, Service, Service,* by Steve Albrecht

Most anyone can start a personal fitness training business. The purpose of this book thus far has been to help guide you through the various stages of starting his own business. While other trainers may have access to the same certifications, equipment, support groups (accountants, lawyers, etc.), marketing, advertising, and even this book, there is only one of you! Through meticulous dedication to customer service, you can distinguish your personal training services from those offered by others.

While the thought of distinguishing one's company seems easy— it is not. Customers have many expectations when they decide to spend their money, and it is your responsibility to exceed the customer's expectations. Simply giving the customers what they want is not enough in a competitive business world.

Chapter 9 discussed the "sphere of influence" factor: the far-reaching number of people a businessperson knows and can refer to a personal training business. Do not forget that customers also have their own "sphere of influence." This "sphere" is a double-edge sword. If customers are happy with your service, they will tell others. But if customers are dissatisfied with your service, they will tell even more people. Consider this: a business can spend roughly 10 times more money trying to attract new customers than retaining current ones. The importance of actively maintaining impeccable customer relations cannot be stated more succinctly than that!

Rules of Customer Service

"Company policies are overhead, customers are profits."
—*How to Drive Your Competition Crazy* by Guy Kawasaki

The quote by Sam Walton at the beginning of this chapter summarizes the importance of customers. Without them, businesses fail—regardless of the product or services being offered. The following is a list of ways for your company to maintain focus on the client:

1. *Be Consistent*—Regardless of a company's philosophy and policies, the most important criterion (from a business standpoint) is that the company provide the client with the services agreed upon. If your company promises "Results for Every Client," you may find yourself with an angry client who failed to lose weight and now wants a refund. In that case, the best thing to do would be to offer a refund because you did not deliver what you promised: results for every client. Granted, you can never know what clients do when they are not receiving one-to-one training. Your job is to try to offer services that satisfy a variety of different training protocols.

2. *Understand the Customer*—Businesses cannot sell their products to everyone. Personal training is a niche service and must be targeted to specific individuals. You might want to target people that:
   - Aren't getting the RESULTS they want.
   - Want to update their program.
   - Are training for a specific goal.
     Examples: • decrease body fat
                • increase strength and flexibility
                • train for a specific sporting event
   - Want to get into better shape
   - Want motivation!

3. *Know What the Customer Wants*—Are your company's hours agreeable? Is there enough variety in pricing schedules? Do the clients prefer same sex trainers? These are questions you should continually ask yourself when operating a business. Business does not remain static, so a business owner's approach to customer service must keep up with the times. What your clients want and feel are important amenities today may be less important, or even obsolete, a couple of years from now.

4. *Give Customers What they Want!*—Customers can be fickle. Remember that they are spending money on personal training services. If there is room for interpretation or improvement, you must provide complementary solutions. Listen to the clients and make sure they are satisfied.

5. *Keep Them Coming Back*—Happy clients are repeat clients. If clients feel that a personal trainer is making a positive impact on their health, they will be more apt to renew their training agreement. If they feel a trainer (or company) goes out of their way to provide excellent service, chances are clients will renew if they can afford it.

Relationship Reinforcers

"Each impression you make will—temporarily, at least—be your last. So make it strong."
—Selling the Invisible, *by Harry Beckwith*

Making clients feel important, recognized, and special plays a large role in the customer service a company provides. Following is a list of ways a company can provide the best customer service possible:

1. *Be Honest*—Without honesty, a company is destined to fail. There are plenty of personal trainers who aren't certified, claim they are, and train individuals for money. For the most part, their working knowledge of physiology and anatomy barely exceeds that of a layperson. Such unethical behavior is bad for the industry and, once exposed, will create distrust with a company's clientele.

2. *Be Responsive*—Generally speaking, every call should be returned within 24 hours. Making someone wait for a callback may result in loss of revenue. Do not let prospects, clients, or professional associates wait. Provide them the same customer service that you demand of others!

3. *Be Trustworthy*—Clients are going to divulge personal information via the initial interview, health history questionnaire, or during their training sessions. Be sure to convey how confidentially this information is held. Otherwise, a company's credibility will be at stake. Trainers should *never* discuss a client's history with anyone without *first* obtaining permission from the client.

4. *Be Prepared*—Clients do not care if trainers see one client per day or ten. What they do care about is that their trainer is prepared with their workout regimen during their allotted training appointment.

5. *Thank you, Thank you, Thank you*—Trainers can never thank clients and prospects enough. Companies should thank clients for choosing their services, thank them for referring their services, thank them for their loyalty, thank them for their dedication, etc. (See Appendix M for an example of a "Thank you for choosing our services" letter.)

6. *Establish Client Retention Procedures*—The art of selling lies in a businessperson's ability to create a relationship with the prospect. People buy from others because they like them. People buy again because a person has continued to be likable, professional, and educated. By establishing Client Retention Procedures, you can maintain a position of visibility and professionalism with each client in a cohesive manner. Retention forms and procedures can be reviewed

weekly to determine if, and how, a company can be of service to its clients. (See Appendix N for a Client Checklist and Retention Procedures.)

"The most important single ingredient in the formula of success is knowing how to get along with people."
—*Theodore Roosevelt*

Reference

Albrecht, S. (1994). Service, Service, *Service: A Secret Weapon for Your Growing Business,* Adams Media Corporation. Holbrook, Massachusetts.

Procedures A to Z

## 11

"Study each point of contact. Then improve each one—significantly."

—Selling the Invisible, *by Harry Beckwith*

"Great things are not done by implulse, but by a

series of small things brought together."

—*Vincent Van Gogh*

"One thing at a time, all things in succession. That which

grows slowly endures."

—*J.G. Holland*

Chapter at a Glance

Checklist of Required Items to Get Started
Phone Calls, Faxes, E-mails, and Letters
Fitness Consultations
Personal Training Packages and Rates
Signing up New Clients
New Client Procedures
Postcards: When to Send Them
Retention Forms and Procedures

The purpose of this chapter is to tie everything together. A company is simultaneously evolving and addressing different issues. Be prepared for the different roles that need to be assumed when operating a business. This chapter will clarify the various responsibilities of owning and managing a personal training operation.

OF NOTE

While a one-person training company can most certainly complete the procedures in this chapter, the responsibilities will be divided between a personal trainer and a Director of Training. Even if your company is a one-person business, you will better understand the delegation of responsibility once the business demands additional trainers.

Checklist of Required Items to Get Started

For a complete list of items to have on hand prior to accepting the first client, see Appendix O. While some items are more important than others, each one on this list helps make the day-to-day operation run smoothly.

Phone Calls, Faxes, E-mails, and Letters

Respond to an inquiry by calling the prospect on the telephone, unless advised to correspond via e-mail or regular mail. If the person is not available, leave a detailed message letting him know who you are, the nature of your call, and how you can be reached (both daytime and evening numbers).

OF NOTE

When leaving messages for prospects to return a call, give them two numbers, a daytime number (typically your office number), and an evening number (cell phone or pager). Let the clients know that they can reach you twenty-four hours a day, seven days a week. This is an important practice because most working professionals may not have discretionary time during the workday to return phone calls. By giving them the option of calling during the evening (or possibly first thing in the early morning) you provide them with an added service: convenience.

When speaking with prospects, use the initial conversation to accomplish one thing: Arrange an appointment for a Fitness Consultation. Do not try to sell them on the phone. Schedule an appointment that fits their schedule.

Fitness Consultations

The purpose of the first training session is to gather the information needed regarding a client's health status, goals, and physical capacity so you can properly design an exercise program.

Before sitting down with a prospect for a FREE fitness consultation, make sure to have the appropriate New Client Forms (Figure 24). If the prospect decides to enroll, have all the forms handy for processing a new client.

New Client Forms	
Personal Training Agreement	(Appendix B)
Health History Questionnaire	(Appendix C)
Informed Consent Agreement	(Appendix F)
Fitness Consultation Form	(Appendix O)
New Client Information Sheet	(Appendix P)
Request for Pre-authorized Payment Program	(Appendix R)
Payment Control Sheet	(Appendix Q)

Figure 24

Personal Training Packages and Rates

Two types of personal training packages that can be offered are the Goal Achievement (a three-month package) and the One-to-One training package (5 or 10 sessions with a personal trainer).

Goal Achievement Program (3-month package)

This package cannot be introduced to prospective clients until they have been pre-qualified. Why? Simply stated, three months is a substantial commitment on the prospect's part. It is a psychological commitment. Will they stick to the program? Do they have the time? Do they have the desire and drive? And it is also a financial commitment. During the closing of the sale, it is important to complete a Fitness Evaluation to know as much about the prospect as possible (Appendix T).

The Goal Achievement Program is designed to ensure optimum results. However, it lasts only twelve weeks and must be presented within the context that most of the prospect's fitness goals will not occur in this short timeframe.

The Goal Achievement Program is an intensive program, with the trainer working with a client two, three, or four times/week for 12 weeks. More often than not, prospects are going to examine this program and scrutinize the expense rather than what the trainer can do for them. A trainer's responsibility is to diffuse the issue of money. Personal trainers must *sell the benefits of exercise.* Describe what people can expect from regular exercise besides a smaller pants or dress size, weight loss, etc.

Other benefits can be added to this list. Of prime importance is that a trainer convey to clients or prospects that no matter what their goal(s) are, change will not occur overnight. People will not lose weight, lower their cholesterol, or gain lean muscle overnight. The Goal Achievement Program will help prospects work towards achieving these changes over time. This, in turn, will help improve the quality of their lives.

One-to-One Training Services (packages of 5 or 10 sessions)

Some prospects are not going to want to work with a trainer for 12 or more weeks. The reason may be financial. Or it could turn out that they do not need qualified attention to make sure they adhere to their program. They may be seeking someone to help create or update a fitness program for them, or educate them on exercises they can perform to help achieve their individual goals.

If clients want to purchase a few sessions—or even a single session— to get started and then work on their own do not change the quality of your service. Educate clients on the benefits of exercise, proper biomechanics, and the components of a complete fitness program.

If you want to increase your client base you must show that you have the knowledge to take clients to any desired level and to work with clients in any capacity they desire. This approach will increase clients' confidence in you and increase the perceived value of personal training services to prospective clientele.

The Group Approach

The group approach is the same training package as one-to-one personal training, except that you are training more than one person per session. Though any pricing schedule can be developed, the typical industry discount for each client of a "group" session is 25% off the individual cost. For example, if two people want to purchase ten sessions individually, at a cost of $450.00 each, they can train together during the same hour ("group training") for $337.50 each (a 25% discount).

During the fitness consultation ask questions regarding whether or not any family members, friends, or co-workers know about the prospect's goals. Listen closely to the answer. If the answer is yes, ask the prospect if that person is a member of a health club. Why? Because this friend, family member, or co-worker may be simply confused by all the equipment in a gym or by the principles of fitness. The result could be that prospects sign up for the group approach merely to have someone they know working out with them. Many people are embarrassed or shy about working with a trainer. Your job during the fitness consultation (and every personal training session thereafter) is to make the clients feel comfortable. Two things happen when clients are put at ease: 1) They concentrate on what you are saying and are not preoccupied by their own fears or embarrassment, and 2) They will have a greater appreciation for your services. This person will not only become a client, but hopefully a repeat client.

Personal Training Rates

Prospective clients are looking to hire your services at a variety of locations: the health club/studio, home, or workplace. The pricing schedule your company offers can be broken down into two categories: on-site and off-site (Appendix U).

By offering less expensive sessions than the One-to-One training packages, the Goal Achievement Program offers prospective clients a financial incentive if they initially decide to sign up for a longer term. However, these sessions must be used within each seven-day period for 12 weeks regardless of the frequency (two, three, or four times per week). For example, if a person signs up for the Fit 2 or Home 2 package, they must train three times during any given week or they will lose whichever sessions are not completed. This is not to say that their training times or days cannot vary if unforeseen circumstances arise. But three sessions must be completed per week with no carryover to the next week. It is important that you convey this to prospective clients before enrolling them. Even if clients miss a few sessions over the course of three months, they will still be ahead financially versus buying ten sessions at a time (the One-to-One training package).

One-to-One training packages are priced higher than the Goal Achievement Program, but they offer clients more flexibility in the scheduling of their appointments. Solo 1 and Solo 3 packages (five sessions) must be used within thirty days of the date of purchase and Solo 2 and Solo 4 packages (ten sessions) must be used within 60 days of the date of purchase.

Important Note

Never deceive any prospective client regarding the pros and cons of training packages. A company's expectations of their trainers should be that the trainers fully inform all clients of the benefits or detriments of each training package. Such ethical and professional behavior will allow clients to make informed decisions and lead to less misunderstanding in the future. Take the time to explain the training packages in great detail and answer any questions that may arise!

Signing up New Clients

Once a client has decided on a training package and is ready to sign up, the paper work is simply a formality. Each new member file must contain certain completed documents for it to be considered complete (see Figure 25).

Each of these new client forms should be filled out completely and placed in a designated location (e.g., the Director of Training's mailbox).

The Health History Questionnaire (HHQ) and Fitness Consultation Form (Appendices E and P) are straightforward in terms of their requirements. The Personal Training Agreement (Appendix D) needs to be filled out according to the program a client wishes to purchase. It has two options: Goal Achievement and One-to-One training. If a client is buying a Solo 1 package, you should fill out the One-to-One training package section of the agreement filling in the number of sessions (5), the cost ($225) (assuming this is your company fee), and the time period (30 days). Each part for the Goal Achievement Program must therefore be written in as "not applicable," or "N/A." This means the client is legally responsible only for the portion that has been completed in the One-to-One portion of the agreement. It is important (using this above example) not to leave the Goal Achievement portion blank after filling in the One-to-One portion. You must put "N/A" wherever charges DO NOT apply!

New Client Checklist

- **Health History Questionnaire (completed)**
- **Fitness Consultation Form (completed)**
- **Personal Training Agreement (signed and dated by client)**
- **Informed Consent (signed, initialed, and dated by client)**
- **Payment Control Sheet (completed by trainer)**
- **EFT Form with voided check or credit card slip (if necessary)**

Figure 25

The Informed Consent Form (Appendix H) must also be signed, initialed, and dated, because this document, combined with the Personal Training Agreement, is legally binding.

OF NOTE

The only time a client is to complete an informed consent but not complete a contract is if there is no money involved or if a trainer waits to process the training fees until the first session is completed. If clients want to train first before paying, they *MUST* complete an informed consent form before having a trainer work with them! A company should have absolutely no exceptions to this rule!

A Request of Pre-Authorized Payment Program Form, or Electronic Funds Transfer (EFT) request (Appendix R), must be completed if a client is purchasing a training package that does not require payment in full.

Although the client will be responsible for the first month up front, a billing company will bill the client for the second and third month. Therefore, a completed EFT form must have attached either a voided check or a voided credit card slip.

Forms of payment

A company can accept payment in cash, check, money order, or credit card. Regardless of the form of payment, a Payment Control Sheet (Appendix S) must be completed and included in the New Client file in order to maintain accurate records of each sale.

Electronic Terminals

An electronic terminal allows companies to accept payment by credit card. If a client is paying by credit card, make sure that the training staff is comfortable and knowledgeable on how to use the credit card terminal.

WARNING!

Starter checks, which do not include the customer's address and phone number, should NOT be accepted as a form of payment!

Procedure

When a client signs up to take personal training services, make sure each legal document is signed and initialed where necessary and that all the forms are complete and together. Do not forget to include the method of payment with these forms! Put this information in a folder while it awaits processing.

Daily Sales Control (DSC) Sheets + Monthly Sales Controls (MSC) Sheets

The first step in processing a new client is recording the method of payment. If you are using a billing company, they will provide you with revenue-tracking forms. It is a good idea to track your company's sales on a daily and monthly basis; this provides you with a system of checks and balances.

Billing companies need more information than just the amount of daily revenue being generated. The DSC requires the new client's name, down payment, amount being financed, total dollar amount, what type of program the client chooses (month-to-month or paid in full), and whether the client is new or renewing. All of this information is faxed or sent electronically to the billing company along with a New Client Information Sheet (Appendix Q).

New Client Procedures

Personal Trainer Responsibilities

Immediately after new clients leave a company's offices, send a Thank You postcard. In addition, 24 hours after a client's first training session the trainer should call and ask how the client feels, give them advice or motivation, and thank them again for choosing the company's services.

In an attempt to gain name recognition, a company can distribute free shirts or tank tops to new clients. Important note: Pay a little more for high quality shirts. Chances are that even if clients are no longer hiring a company's services, they will be wearing the shirts while exercising. A shirt that is falling apart due to poor quality reflects poorly on any company!

Director of Training Responsibilities

After receiving the folder containing a new client's information the Director of Training should also send a Thank You letter. In addition, he should add the new client's information to the company's client information lists and database. By inputting this information in a database, business owners have the option of including the client in a variety of future mailings.

When a company gives something substantial (e.g., shirts and tank tops) to new clients, they make the people feel like they are a part of an exclusive group. This act of giving also works as an advertising tool for the personal training company. Personal trainers can supplement their clients' training programs by giving gift subscriptions to health and fitness publications. This way, your clientele will be reminded of just how much your company cares (up to 12 times annually).

Postcards: When to Send Them

Postcards can be sent out to prospective clients, current clients, former clients, and vendors. Any occasion that has some business importance can be handled either via a postcard or letter. Listed below are examples for each occasion.

New Client

"Thank you for choosing [Your company name] personal training services. I look forward to working with you and helping you achieve your fitness goals."

Re-testing for Fitness Evaluation

"[x] months have passed since your last fitness evaluation. Please give me a call at your earliest convenience to schedule your next evaluation."

Special Event (marriage, new job, promotion, relocating, etc.)

"Congratulations on [new job, promotion, etc.]. Keep up the hard work! We look forward to seeing you in the gym."

Thank You for Renewing

"Thank you for renewing your personal training sessions. I look forward to your future progress."

Monthly Updates and/or Support

"[Client's name], you had great workouts this past month. Keep up the good work. I'll see you at our next scheduled appointment."

Referrals (current clientele)

"Do you know of anyone who might benefit from our personal training services? [Your company name] offers gift certificates for referrals. Give the gift of fitness and we'll reward you with a free gift!"

Thanking a Client for Referrals

"Thank you for referring [Client's name] to us. Your support of our services is greatly appreciated."

Client Birthdays

"Happy Birthday from all of us at [Your company name]!"

Holiday Postcard

"[Whichever occasion] from all of us at [Your company name]!"

Client Leaving Personal Training Business

"Thank you for choosing [Your company name]. Good luck with your program."

Postcards are an effective way to keep in touch with current clients as well as prospective or former clients. Postcards show that a company cares enough about customer service to take the time to write them. From a business perspective, postcards also serve as marketing tools: They keep a company's name in front of a target audience.

Retention Forms and Procedures

Service-oriented companies need to take pride in their customer service. In order to keep track of customer service and make sure clients are 100% satisfied, companies should prepare "Retention Forms" for *each* client (Appendix N). Retention forms guarantee that a company stays in touch with its clientele and continues to provide quality service. Both the clients' personal trainers and the Director of Training are responsible for corresponding with the clients for the following reasons:

- To make sure the workouts are satisfactory (phone calls, questionnaires, testimonials, etc.)
- To provide feedback on progress (monthly postcards, phone calls, and letters)
- To inform and educate (*ACE FitnessMatters*, applicable magazine or newspaper articles sent)
- To improve your company's personal training services (questionnaire, phone calls, and letters).

Each time a company corresponds with a client they are providing a service. People like to be recognized and thought of as important.

Once a week, each trainer should make a "Weekly To-Do List" (Appendix V). This ensures that each client is being properly serviced. If there is any reason for a company to correspond with its clientele (via letter, phone call, postcard, questionnaire, etc.), this will help ensure that the correspondence is completed. All trainers must go through their respective "Current Retention Form" folders and make sure the retention procedures are carried out in a timely fashion. Completed "Weekly To-Do List" (with any applicable postcards or other correspondence) can be placed in the Director of Training's mailbox.

The Director of Training checks each personal trainer's "Weekly To-Do List" and double checks to make sure everything is correct. If any errors are made, the Director describes the action that needs to be taken and returns the weekly list to the trainer for completion.

A company's retention procedures cover correspondence from the moment clients meet with trainers for a fitness consultation to follow-up processes after the clients discontinue their personal training.

Summary

Remember, personal training is a health and fitness profession. When people buy personal training services, they are not guaranteeing how long they will work with you. Chances are that if clients do not achieve their fitness goals, they will terminate their relationship with your company. Yet, if you build a rapport with the clients and they feel comfortable with you, they will probably become repeat clients. A company should never compromise its quality of service. If you are trustworthy, on time, and friendly, clients will want to work with you again. Clients may not sign up for successive sessions, but if they felt that their money was well spent, liked you and felt you were knowledgeable, they will either train again or send referrals.

Reference

Beckwith, H. (1997). *Selling the Invisible: A Field Guide to Modern Marketing*. New York. Warner Books.

## 12

Future Growth

"This is not the end. It is not even the beginning of the end.
But it is, perhaps, the end of the beginning."
—*Winston Churchill*

"Don't bother just to be better than
your contemporaries or predecessors.
Try to be better than yourself."
—*William Faulkner*

"My way of fighting the
competition is the
positive approach.
Stress your own
strengths, emphasize
quality, service, cleanliness, and
value, and the competition will wear
itself out trying to keep up."
—*Ray Kroc, founder and late chairman of McDonald's*

Chapter at a Glance

Planning for the Future
Additional Streams of Revenue
Approaching Corporations
Final Note

Planning for the Future

"Four steps to achievement: plan purposefully, prepare prayerfully, proceed positively, pursue persistently."
— *William A. Ward*

Before you as a business owner can consider increasing the size of your business (number of trainers, number of locations, services offered, etc.) you should have a firm understanding of each department within your company. This is not to say that you need to be an expert in each department. But you should have an understanding of where the fiscal health of the company is at all times.

By now you should know the steps in starting a personal training business. This is by no means the end of the journey. A business does not remain static. It is a dynamic entity that is constantly changing and evolving. To a large degree, it is the business owner's responsibility to place his company in an "environment" (i.e., marketplace) where it not only survives, but flourishes. This is easier said than done. James Collins and Jerry Porras (1997), in their book *Built to Last*, explain how visionary companies provide for their future.

"...the most fundamental distinguishing characteristic of the most enduring and successful corporations is that they preserve a cherished core ideology while simultaneously stimulating progress and change in everything that isn't part of their core ideology. Put another way, they distinguish their timeless core values and enduring core purpose (which should never change) from their operating practices and business strategies (which should be changing constantly in response to a changing world). In truly great companies, change is a constant, but not the only constant. They understand the difference between what should never change and what should be open for change...." p. 220

Additional Streams of Revenue

Once a company becomes profitable offering personal training services, it can channel some energy into peripheral services that will help increase annual revenues. These additional streams of revenue can be tied to personal training (e.g., running programs, walking programs, self-defense). Or they can be products or services that help increase company awareness and revenues (e.g., web site revenues, clothing sales, fitness-related group outings). A few examples of such programs, services, and products are outlined below to help illustrate how business owners can make money while promoting their company at the same time.

Running Programs/ Walking Programs

Running and walking programs are great ways to help generate interest in activity from different kinds of people: those who exercise and those who normally do not. Group activities bring individuals together. As a group, many people are more likely to maintain a consistent exercise program as a direct result of peer support. A running program can be devised to help people prepare for a local race (10K, 10 mile, half-marathon, or a marathon). You can align yourself with charities to help raise public awareness and also increase the likelihood of receiving charitable donations. Such alliances produce exposure that money cannot buy. The most important exposure generated is public *good will.* Local communities look at such programs with admiration and respect. Secondly, companies can use their charitable programs to help market themselves through press releases, direct mailings, newsletters, web pages, etc. When attached to a charitable cause, a company is more likely to receive positive feedback from the community and their target customers.

Self-Defense Classes and Other Seminars

Business owners can utilize their unique education and experiences by offering classes or seminars. If the offerings are specialized enough (self-defense, golf, tennis, etc.) you can offer a fee-for-service class or seminar. For an idea of how much to charge and how to determine costs associated with such offerings, see "Measuring Profitability" in Chapter 5.

Fitness Products

Fitness professionals have the ability to present their customers a large variety of health and fitness–related products beyond personal training. Company owners can market and sell numerous items (e.g., clothing, fitness equipment, and a company newsletter). You can use your current client base as a start to offer your products through direct mail campaigns. Or you can utilize your company Web site.

Web Site

Chapter 8 discussed the importance of having a presence on the Internet. Having an Internet presence allows companies to market themselves, provide services, information, products, and generate additional revenue. Some of the more well-known vehicles for this are online personal training services (updated regularly), fitness products (e.g., clothing, equipment, books, newsletters), and information (members-only section).

Approaching Corporations

Personal training businesses should not limit their services to the residential market. Targeting corporations is a great way for personal training businesses to expose themselves to a larger audience at a fraction of the advertising cost. Sending posters, flyers, postcards, or e-mails to a corporate headquarters is an inexpensive method of reaching a large target audience. You can also offer their personal training services on-site (if the company allows freelance trainers and also has the facilities for such services). Use corporations as a springboard to help expand your company. When planning for the future it is important to put your company's name and services in front of as many prospects as possible. Catering to the corporate world can help achieve such growth.

Final Note

Never lose sight of your company's philosophy. Preach this philosophy to employees, clientele, and vendors. Putting clients ahead of profits will prove rewarding and establish your company as a reputable health and fitness service provider.

"No one succeeds without effort...Those who succeed owe their success to their perseverance."

– *Ramana Maharshi*

Reference

Collins, J.C. and Porras, J.I. (1997). *Built to Last: Successful Habits of Visionary Companies*. New York. Harper Collins Books.

Appendices

Note: Before incorporating any of these form letters into your personal training business, consult with a lawyer in the state where you will be conducting business, to confirm any legal relevance they contain.

APPENDIX A

Certification Organizations

American Council on Exercise (ACE)
5820 Oberlin Dr., Suite 102
San Diego, CA 92121
Phone: 800.825.3636
Web Address: www.acefitness.org

American College of Sport Medicine (ACSM)
P.O. Box 1440
Indianapolis, IN 46206-1440
Phone: 800.486.5643 or 317.637.9200
Web Address: www.acsm.org

National Strength and Conditioning Association Certification Commission (NSCA)
1640 L St., Suite G
Lincoln, NE 68508
Phone: 800.815.6826 or 402.476.6669
Web Address: www.nsca-cc.org

APPENDIX B

INDEPENDENT CONTRACTOR AGREEMENT

THIS INDEPENDENT CONTRACTOR AGREEMENT (this "Agreement") is made this ___ day of _____, 20____, by and between "ABC," a Your State corporation (the "Company"), and PERSONAL TRAINING BUSINESS, INC., a Your State corporation, (the "Trainer").

As used herein, the term "agents, employees, servants, or subcontractors" shall include Your Name, and any other existing or future employees, agents, servants, or subcontractors of the Trainer.

IN CONSIDERATION of the mutual promises set forth herein, it is agreed by and between the Company and the Trainer the following:

1. DESCRIPTION OF SERVICES

A.   The Trainer will provide personal training and fitness consulting services as provided in this Agreement (collectively, the "Training Services").

2. INDEPENDENT CONTRACTOR

A.   It is understood and agreed between the parties that the Trainer is an independent contractor in the performance of each and every part of this Agreement and that the Trainer is solely liable for all labor and expenses in connection with this Agreement.

B.   Neither the Trainer nor any of its agents, employees, servants or subcontractors shall be deemed to be the employee, agent, servant or subcontractor of the Company. Trainer shall perform this Agreement as an independent contractor and nothing herein shall be construed to be inconsistent with this relationship or status. The Company shall not be liable for the acts of the Trainer's agents, employees, servants, or subcontractors during the performance of this Agreement.

C.   In the performance of all matters relevant to this Agreement, Trainer is an independent contractor with the sole authority to control and direct the performance of the details of the Training Services provided to Trainer's clients. The Company shall have no authority to control or direct the performance of the details of the Training Services provided to the clients of the Trainer. The Company shall have no authority to control or direct the performance of the details of the Training Services provided to the clients of the Trainer's agents, employees, servants, or subcontractors.

The Company shall use the Training Services of the Trainer exclusively at the Company's Virginia location. Use of other trainers and/or training companies at the Company's Virginia location shall constitute a material breach of this Agreement.

Trainer agrees to comply with all federal, state and municipal laws, rules and regulations that are now or may in the future become applicable to Trainer or Trainer's business, equipment and employees engaged in operations covered by this Agreement or accruing out of the performance of such operations. Trainer is not to be considered an employee of the Company for any purpose, and the employees of Trainer are not entitled to any of the benefits that the Company provides for the Company's employees.

D.   Trainer acknowledges the Trainer's obligation to obtain appropriate liability insurance coverage for the benefit of the Trainer, the Trainer's employees, and the Trainer's clients. Trainer will carry, for the duration of this Agreement, insurance coverage in an amount not less than One Million Dollars ($1,000,000.00).

E.   The Company shall keep the Company's Facilities, as defined below, and all equipment used by the Trainer, its employees, agents, and/or subcontractors, if any, furnished, rented, or loaned to Trainer by the Company (the "Facility Equipment") in a reasonably safe condition. The Trainer shall not be responsible or be held liable for any injury or damage to person or property resulting from the Company's Facilities, or from the failure of any Facility Equipment used by Trainer or any of Trainer's employees, agents or subcontractors. The Company shall indemnify and hold harmless the Trainer, its employees, agents, and/or subcontractors, if any, against all liability or loss, and against all claims, damages, expenses, or actions based upon or arising out of damage or injury, including death, to persons or property caused by the Company's Facilities or from the failure of any Facility Equipment used by the Trainer, its employees, agents, and/or subcontractors, if any.

F.   The Trainer shall indemnify and hold harmless the Company against any loss, claims, or actions based upon or arising out of damage or injury, including death, to persons or property caused by or sustained in connection with the performance of Training Services by the Trainer, its employees, agents, and/or subcontractors, to the Trainer's clients or to the clients of the Trainer's employees, agents, and/or subcontractors, under this Agreement.

G.   Trainer shall indemnify and hold harmless the Company against all liability and loss in connection with, and shall assume full liability for, payment of all federal, state, and local taxes or contributions imposed or required under employment insurance, social security, and income tax laws, with respect to Trainer's employees engaged in the performance of Training Services under this Agreement.

H.   Trainer agrees to maintain at Trainer's expense, such insurance as will fully protect the Trainer from any and all claims under any worker's compensation act that may arise from operations carried on under this Agreement, either by Trainer, any subcontractor or by anyone directly or indirectly engaged or employed by the Trainer.

I.   The Trainer certifies that the Trainer's employees, agents, and/or subcontractors if any, who perform Training Services under this Agreement, have a background in Personal Training, are certified by an accredited organization, are CPR certified, are covered by liability insurance of at least one million dollars ($1,000,000.00), are current in personal training techniques, and are willing to provide services to the Company based on this background.

J.   Trainer, its employees, agents, and/or subcontractors if any, who perform Training Services under this Agreement, and/or who solicit Training Services at the Company's Facilities, agree, while providing Training Services and while soliciting Training Services at the Company's Facilities, under this Agreement, to wear uniforms which are similar to the uniforms worn by ABC's Gym employees: provided, however, that Trainer, its employees, agent, and/or subcontractors, if any, shall not wear any item of clothing which contains the ABC's Gym logo or the logo worn by ABC's Gym employees.

K.   Trainer shall furnish qualified people to provide Training Services under this Agreement. Trainer shall at all times enforce strict discipline and maintain good order among those engaged by it for such Training Services, and shall cause such workers to observe all reasonable fire prevention and safety rules and regulations in force at the site of the training. Trainer shall not employ any unfit person or anyone not skilled in the training assigned. Trainer and its representatives shall dress and present themselves in a professional manner.

L.   Trainer agrees to be responsible for its own supplies including, but not limited to copy paper, business machine usage, forms, business cards, contracts, and any specified uniforms. Trainer shall not use the Company's employees to provide Training Services under this Agreement, at the Company's Facilities. Trainer is not responsible for, and shall not be obligated to provide orientation training provided by the Company to ABC's Gym members.

3. CLIENTS

A.   All clients currently training under the supervision of the Trainer, members of ABC's Gym (the "Existing Clients"), shall be deemed to be the Trainer's clients upon the execution of this Agreement. All clients who hire the Trainer, its employees, agents, and/or subcontractors, if any, subsequent to the execution of this Agreement, whether members or non-members of ABC's Gym, shall be deemed to be the Trainer's clients. In the event of the termination of this Agreement, Trainer shall have the right to continue to use its clients, whether members or non-members of ABC's Gym.

4. COLLECTION OF FEES

A.   The Trainer will collect fees directly from the Trainer's clients at a rate set by the Trainer. The Company shall have no authority to control or direct the fees charged by the Trainer.

5. PAYMENT TO COMPANY

A. The Trainer agrees to pay the Company "$X.XX."

The monies paid by the Trainer to the Company pursuant to this Section 5, shall be due and payable on or before the first day of each and every calendar month, without set-off or demand.

The failure of the Trainer to perform its obligations under this Section 5 shall be deemed a material breach of this Agreement. The Company shall have the right, at reasonable times and upon reasonable notice, to inspect Trainer's books at Trainer's place of business to ensure Trainer is in compliance with this Section 5.

6. TERM

A. The initial term of this Agreement shall be for one year and shall commence on _____ and shall terminate on_____, (the "Initial Term"), provided however, that either party may terminate this Agreement as provided in paragraphs 7 and 13, below. This Agreement may be extended for an additional one year (the "Extension Term") beyond the Initial Term or any Extension Term only by the written agreement of both parties prior to the expiration of the Initial Term or any Extension Term.

7. TERMINATION OF AGREEMENT

A. Either party may cancel this Agreement on sixty (60) days advance written notice. Notice of cancellation shall be by hand delivery or by certified mail, postage prepaid, return receipt requested to the addresses provided in paragraph 13.

8. ENTIRE AGREEMENT

A. This Agreement contains the entire agreement of the parties and there are no other promises or conditions or any other agreement whether oral or written. This Agreement supersedes any prior or contemporaneous written or oral agreements between the Company and the Trainer.

9. AMENDMENT

A. This Agreement may be modified or amended, if the amendment is made in writing and is signed by both parties.

10. SEVERABILITY

A. If any provision of this Agreement shall be held to be invalid or unenforceable for any reason, the remaining provisions shall continue to be valid and enforceable.

11. WAIVER OF CONTRACTUAL RIGHT

A. The failure of either party to enforce any provision of this Agreement shall not be construed as a waiver or limitation of that party's right to subsequently enforce and compel strict compliance with every provision of this Agreement. The failure of either party to enforce any provision of this Agreement shall not be construed as a waiver or limitation of that party's right to exercise any right in the event of any subsequent default. In the event of a default hereunder, the non-defaulting party shall give the defaulting party written notice of such default and five (5) business days to cure such default prior to exercising any rights hereunder.

12. APPLICABLE LAW

A.   This Agreement shall be governed by the laws of the Commonwealth of Virginia without regard to conflicts of law.

13. NOTICES

A.   All notices required or permitted under this Agreement shall be in writing and shall be deemed delivered when delivered by hand or deposited in the United States mail, certified mail, postage prepaid, return receipt requested, addressed as follows:

Company:
Attention:
Address:

Trainer:
Attention:
Address:

14. HEADINGS

A.   The headings used in this Agreement are for convenience only and do not form part of this Agreement and are not intended to interpret, define or limit the scope, extent or intent of this Agreement or any provision hereof.

15. BINDING EFFECT

A.   This Agreement shall inure to the benefit of and be binding upon the respective parties, their heirs, executors, administrators, successors in interest and assigns.

16. ADVERTISING

A.   Nothing in this Agreement shall prohibit the Trainer from advertising its Training Services outside the Company's Virginia location.
Personal Training Business, Inc.

BY: BY:

TITLE: TITLE:

DATE: DATE:

APPENDIX C

Sample Business Plan

Vision/Mission

Present Situation

Personal Training Business, Inc. was founded in 2001. The company provides quality one-to-one fitness training to individuals in Anytown, USA, and surrounding areas.

Market and Sales Environment

The past decade has shown a shift to healthier lifestyles. As such, the health club industry has seen tremendous growth. The future growth potential for ABC's Gym is excellent because the prevalence of physical activity in the United States is estimated at only 10%. In addition, only 5% of the U.S. population is familiar with the appropriate intensity, duration, and frequency of physical activity to achieve cardiopulmonary fitness. Combining these two statistics makes it readily apparent that there is not only a need for health facilities such as ABC's Gym, but also for professionally educated and certified fitness trainers.

The Company's Mission

Our goal is to increase the general population's level of fitness. We plan on providing such service by entering into an exclusive agreement with ABC's Gym to provide one-to-one fitness training to their members and other Personal Training Business, Inc. clients. We are a company dedicated to providing service of consistently high quality and establishing long-term relationships with our clients. We aim to be known as one of the premiere one-to-one fitness training companies in the United States.

Services

The company offers one-to-one fitness training to all individuals interested in improving their health and well-being.

Personal Training Business, Inc. aims to provide an instructional, educational, and enjoyable alternative to individuals interested in improving their health. We believe our first responsibility is to our clients.

Strategic Goals

At present, Personal Training Business, Inc. is limited in the services it can provide its clients. In order for Personal Training Business, Inc. to attain the vision described in our mission statement, the following primary strategic goals need to be achieved:

Market:

Year One:

By April 2002, Personal Training Business, Inc. projects to have an active base of over 30 clients, with a projected minimum of three personal trainers at the Anytown facility.

Year Two:

By April 2002, Personal Training Business, Inc. projects to have an active base of over 70 clients with a projected minimum of six personal trainers at ABC's three health clubs.

Years Three through Five:

Between years three through five, Personal Training Business, Inc. projects to have an active base of over 100 clients with a projected minimum of 9 trainers at ABC's three facilities. In addition, Personal Training Business, Inc. plans to expand into any new facilities that open during these subsequent years. For each new facility that opens, the Personal Training Business, Inc. will project goals similar to Year One as stated above.

Sales:

Year One:

By April 2002, Personal Training Business, Inc. will increase the membership enrollment of ABC's Gym by 16, with new one-to-one clients and, by doing so, will generate approximately $3,000 of annual revenue from one-to-one training plus an additional $9,966 in membership fees.* The remaining 14 clients will come from existing members of the first club. This will generate approximately $3,500 in annual revenue for training fees.*

*Based on the assumption that each client will train an average of two times per week ($3.00 profit/per session). Also, the dollar value reflects four new clients every quarter for a year. The membership dues are based on yearly dues of $622.88 ($299 down, $26.99 a month).

**Based on the addition of one client per month for a year. Also, based on an average of two training sessions a week ($6.00 profit/per session).

Year Two:

Personal Training Business, Inc. will increase the membership enrollment by 19. By doing so, we will generate an additional $4,000 in training revenue and an additional $11,500 in membership fees. Twenty-one members of ABC's Gym will become clients of Personal Training Business, Inc., thereby generating $5,200 in training fees. In total over two years, fitness training will generate $15,700 for ABC's Gym and new memberships will have brought in an additional $21,000.

Years Three through Five:

Personal Training Business, Inc. will increase its clientele at the three facilities by 25, for a total of 100 in a 3-5 year period. Twelve of these members will be new, generating new annual revenue of $2,250 in fitness training fees and $7,400 in membership fees. Thirteen of these 25 clients will be ABC's Gym members. They will account for $3,000 in training fees.

Totals for the five-year period are as follows:

New Membership fees:	$28,000
Training Fees (ABC's Gym members)	$11,700
Training Fees (New members)	$ 9,250
Total:	$48,950

Company Overview

Legal Business Description

The legal name of the company is Personal Training Business, Inc. The legal form of the business is a Sub S Corporation. The business location is Your Address, Anytown, USA.

Management Team

Our management team consists of an individual whose experience in the health and fitness industry spans more than ten years.

Your Name
President
Education:
   Include a brief description of your education and certifications.
Responsibilities:
   Develops and maintains the vision of the company. Oversees all marketing, personal training, finances, and client service.

Staffing

Personal Training Business, Inc. recognizes that additional staff is required to properly support our growth while maintaining a high level of quality services. Currently, Personal Training Business, Inc. is composed of one trainer; five trainers will be required to meet the demands of the projected market over the next year.

Fitness Trainers

Requirements:
   Undergraduate degree in related field, or certification from a nationally recognized agency. Current CPR certification is also required.

Responsibilities:
To provide quality one-to-one fitness training.
Accountant
Jane Doe
100 Anywhere Street
City, State, Zip Code
Phone 555.555.5555 Fax 555.777.7777

Product Strategy

Regular physical exercise performed by apparently healthy individuals leads to enhancement and maintenance of muscular strength, muscular endurance, and flexibility. Personal Training Business, Inc. provides quality one-to-one fitness training to members of ABC's Gym, and individuals in surrounding areas. Each training sessions lasts 60 minutes and consists of four components:

- warm-up and cool-down
- flexibility training
- strength training
- aerobic training

By incorporating each of these components into the workout regime, Personal Training Business, Inc. is providing a safe, effective, and comprehensive approach to fitness.

Our company's commitment to excellence does not end with one-to-one training sessions. Currently, Personal Training Business, Inc. is developing a quarterly newsletter that will be distributed to all of our clients and those on our mailing lists. Included in this newsletter will be articles on health and fitness, relevant tips on exercise and diet, upcoming activities, etc. We are using the newsletter as a way of informing our clients and readership of important information within the health and fitness field. Another product the company is developing is an exercise video.

By presenting our product through these media, Personal Training Business, Inc. aims to establish itself as a leader in the health and fitness industry. Other avenues of promotion include fitness seminars, appearances on radio talk shows and local television, and articles on health and fitness issues to be published by local newspapers. Such a strategy will also benefit ABC's Gym because every time we advertise our one-to-one fitness training, we will be directly promoting ABC's Gym. This arrangement presents ABC's Gym with free advertising, word of mouth, and the potential for new membership enrollments.

Market Analysis

Market Definition

The health and fitness industry has grown dramatically in the past 10 years. Public awareness of the importance of proper exercise and diet has been improved through many public and private agencies — most notably the President's Council on Physical Fitness and Sport.

> "A sedentary lifestyle constitutes the greatest single risk to the collective hearts of America," —Center for Disease Control, U.S. Public Health Service.

> "For the first time, we have scientific evidence to support what has always seemed true: regular exercise helps prevent many diseases, lengthens life span, and improves quality of life," —James Rippe, M.D., Director, Exercise Physiology Laboratory, University of Massachusetts Medical School, 1991.

Market Description

Personal Training Business, Inc. and ABC's Gym operate in Anytown, USA and target both households and businesses in the following areas:
 • *List neighboring communities where you are willing to travel for training sessions.*

Market Size and Trends

Anytown, USA, and its surrounding communities, is a large and economically healthy area. According to the Any County Office of Management and Budget (1994), the population within a 4-mile radius, at the intersection of Route 1 and Route 2, is 80,587. The median family income of this same radius is $95,000. In addition, the average daily number of vehicles that pass in front of ABC's Gym is 53,000. As a Central Business District, Anytown's total office space is ranked 15th nationally, with more office space than Houston, Miami, New Orleans, San Diego, and St. Louis.

Strengths and Weaknesses

The one-to-one training offered by Personal Training Business, Inc. at ABC's Gym has a distinct advantage over the competition in terms of recognition. ABC's Gym is an international franchise with over 5,000 locations in the U.S. alone. As such, ABC's Gym's first-class facilities have created mass appeal. By providing quality fitness training, Personal Training Business, Inc. will exemplify the standards the American public has come to expect from ABC's Gym, Inc.

One inherent weakness is the anonymity surrounding the one-to-one fitness training at the Anytown facility. During the next five years, one-to-one fitness training with Personal Training Business, Inc. will establish itself as a leader in the industry. It will also prove to be a highly profitable venture for the owners of ABC's Gym. ABC's Gym will further solidify its reputation as the premiere gym of the area because of its first-class facilities and first-class personal fitness training capabilities.

Marketing Plan

Personal Training Business, Inc. distinguishes itself from other training companies and independent contractors in terms of education, certification, and quality of service.

Meeting ABC's Gym's Needs

Personal Training Business, Inc. is a highly motivated company eager to provide the best service possible to the present and future members of ABC's Gym. Although many health club facilities have their own personal training department, Personal Training Business, Inc. can provide a more ideal environment by performing the following:

- Increasing overall revenue generated to date
- Maintaining sole responsibility for one-to-one fitness training, which decreases the amount of employee dollars spent to oversee such a department and, as a result, provides the gym owner with an added convenience
- Limiting the gym's liability
- Increasing the professional nature of the gym
- Increasing membership

Advertising, Public Relations, and Promotion

Personal Training Business, Inc.'s marketing strategy is to design and promote fitness training in a professional and organized manner so that the company becomes a leading expert in the health and fitness industry. The following summary outline highlights the market programs and specific implementation strategies planned:

1. *Public Relations:* Personal Training Business, Inc. plans to appear on radio talk shows, meet with local interest and professional groups, and write articles, books, and press releases to systematically position itself as a leader in the health and fitness industry. By doing so, we will generate significant ongoing media coverage that will always include the name ABC's Gym.

2. *Advertising:* Materials will be developed and utilized that promote the uniqueness and quality of Personal Training Business, Inc./ ABC's Gym. Personal Training Business, Inc. plans to sell its services through several channels. The determining factors in choosing these channels

are quality, service, and effectiveness in targeting specific customer markets.

Key competition uses similar distribution channels. Our mix of distribution channels will give us the advantage of targeting specific customers. Following is a list of possible channels:

- Newspapers and Magazines

    This avenue is the #1 use of small business marketing money. By using coupons in ads, creating a sense of urgency, emphasizing the word FREE, and using repetition toward a specific consumer niche, Personal Training Business, Inc. plans on generating a substantial number of new clients.

    Personal Training Business, Inc. plans to advertise in local newspapers because the circulation of these periodicals covers our target group. These periodicals include: *provide a list of all local newspapers.*

- Classified Ads

    Less expensive than full ads, we will place classified ads in such magazines as the *Local News* and the *City News*.

    "Sixty-one percent of Americans read magazines from the back to the front, so an economical classified ad will have a decent shot at being read" —Levinson and Godin [1994] *The Guerrilla Marketing Handbook*

- Yellow Pages

    The Yellow Pages is distributed to every household and used by people who are serious about buying/using specific products— it is directional advertising.

- Radio

    In depth cost analysis has not been conducted to date, but bartering our services to get a disk jockey in shape can be used to get ample amounts of airtime. Using radio is an excellent vehicle because adults eighteen and older listen to the radio for approximately three hours each day [Edwards, Edwards, and Douglas (1991) *Getting Business to Come to You*].

- Company Newsletter

    A newsletter is an excellent way to convey information that might otherwise be difficult to report to the client, such as awards the company has received, or some outstanding facts about Personal Training Business, Inc. or its clients. Also, it can contain anecdotes, recipes, industry news, jokes, health and fitness information, etc.

- Circulars

    "For the money, circulars are one of the most powerful of the guerrilla marketing weapons. They are pure power and pure economy" [Levinson and Godin (1994) *The Guerrilla Marketing Handbook*].

- Customer Mailing Lists

   A great way to keep existing clients is by sending greeting cards, birthday cards, relevant articles, thank you notes, newsletters, and/or magazine subscriptions.

- First Class– Lifelong Learning Center

   This is an independently owned non-profit adult education center located in Washington, D.C. Since 1984, 200,000 people have attended their short-term, non-credit classes. Personal Training Business, Inc. can offer classes on a wide array of health and fitness topics.

- Direct Mail Postcards
- Brochures
- Seminars

   A monthly seminar at the Anytown facility for new members will be held. The seminar will present information on beginning an exercise program. Items discussed will include proper warm-up and stretching, free weights versus machines, aerobic and anaerobic activity, proper cool-down, injury prevention, and other gym facts. These seminars will be free to all members and will provide the gym owners an added professional service to offer their new member clientele. Personal Training Business, Inc. will use the seminars as a way of generating publicity, establishing credibility, and enrolling new clients (from whom ABC's Gym would receive an ongoing fee).

- Networking with Physicians, Therapists, and Dieticians
- Testimonials and Endorsements from Existing Clients

Operations, Management, and Organization

Operations

The core of Personal Training Business, Inc.'s strategic concept is one-to-one fitness training. ABC's Gym provides an opportunity to expand the company's existing clientele and, in turn, increase the profits of ABC's Gym.

Agreement with ABC's Gym

Allowing Personal Training Business, Inc. exclusive contracting rights will produce a profit (see Financials, below) with no responsibility or managing effort on the part of any ABC's Gym officer. Personal Training Business, Inc. will assume all sales, marketing, promotion, certification, and liability responsibilities in an effort to increase the revenue ABC's Gym currently receives from personal fitness training.

Management

The company's one principal is:

Your Name

President, Vice President, Secretary, Treasurer

Provide a brief personal biography, including your education, certifications, how long you have been in the fitness industry, and your personal accomplishments.

To date, Your Name is the only employee of Personal Training Business, Inc. His curriculum vitae is included in Attachment A. When not training his clients at the Anytown facility, Your Name is working on a company newsletter and Web page.

Ownership

The ownership of the company is as follows:

Shares	(%)
Your Name	100

Additionally, Personal Training Business, Inc. has an advisory board of individuals experienced in the health and fitness field. Among them are:

Include brief biographies of your advisors, usually members of the health care industry.

Financials

The financials were introduced briefly in the "Vision/Mission" section. The strategic goals mentioned in the "Vision/Mission" section highlighted the amounts profited in years 1,2, and 3-5. Below, the financial goals are established as profits for ABC's Gym. Note that the profits from one-to-one fitness training are broken down into three categories:

- Current ABC's Gym members
- Personal Training Business, Inc. clients who join ABC's Gym
- Personal Training Business, Inc. clients who *do not* join ABC's Gym

Each category will contain projected earnings for a range of training sessions (broken down by month) and the projected earnings for each of these ranges for one year.

Current ABC's Gym members

Fee structure:

Number of Sessions	1-9	10-19	20+
Fee per Session	$40	$35	$30

ABC's fee:

Number of Sessions	1-9	10-19	20+
Fee per Session	$8	$7	$6

Projected Earnings

Faced with choosing a training package, most clients choose 20 or more sessions.* As a result, the following projected earnings will reflect a hypothetical average fee charge of $32.50. ABC's Gym's hypothetical fee is calculated at $6.50 per session. Note that we base our projections on training sessions varying in number from 20 per month to 120 per month per trainer.**

* Based on my experience with my past and present clients.

** Dollar value assumes each trainer trains for a full twelve months when agreement with ABC's Gym is reached.

Monthly

# of sessions	ABC's Gym Earnings
20	$130
40	$260
80	$520
120	$780

Year One (one trainer)

# of sessions	ABC's Gym Earnings
240	$1,560
480	$3,120
960	$6,240
1440	$9,360

Year One (two trainers)

# of sessions	ABC's Gym Earnings
480	$3,120
960	$6,240
1440	$9,360
2880	$18,720

Year One (three trainers)

# of sessions	ABC's Gym Earnings
720	$4,680
1440	$9,360
2880	$18,720
4320	$28,080

Personal Training Business, Inc. Clients Who Join ABC's Gym

Fee structure:

Number of Sessions	1-9	10-19	20+
Fee per Session	$40	$35	$30

ABC's fee:

Number of Sessions	1-9	10-19	20+
Fee per Session	$4	$3.50	$3

Projected Earnings

Again, the projected cost of each training session is hypothetically $32.50. Therefore, the fee paid to ABC's Gym is hypothetically $6.50. The following projected earnings are based on Personal Training Business, Inc.'s projected enrollment of 16 new clients. These projections assume that each new member receives one full-year of fitness training. The annual membership fee of $622.88 is based on $299 down and $26.99 a month. Sales are generated from both fitness training and new membership fees.

Fitness Training

Monthly

# of sessions	ABC's Gym Earnings
20	$65
40	$130
80	$260
120	$390

Year One (one trainer)

# of sessions	ABC's Gym Earnings
240	$780
480	$1,560
960	$3,120
1440	$4,680

Year One (two trainers)

# of sessions	ABC's Gym Earnings
480	$1,560
960	$3,120
1440	$4,680
2880	$9,360

Year One (three trainers)

# of sessions	ABC's Gym Earnings
840	$2,340
1440	$4,680
2880	$9,360
4320	$14,040

New Membership Fees

16 new members at an annual cost of $622.88 = $9,966.08

Personal Training Business, Inc. Clients who do not join ABC's Gym

Fee structure:

1 Month

Number of Sessions	8 (minimum)	12	16
Fee per Session	$50	$50	$50

ABC's Gym's Earnings

8 sessions	12 sessions	16 sessions
$120	$180	$240

By allowing the client to train with Personal Training Business, Inc. without joining the gym, ABC's Gym is recovering the $80 monthly membership fee plus an additional $5, $8.33, and $10 for 8, 12, and 16 sessions respectively. This payment of $80 gives ABC's Gym a 54% profit over the $51.91 monthly fee (based on a yearly membership fee of $299 down, $26.99 a month).

3 Months

Number of Sessions	24 (minimum)	36	48
Fee per Session	$45	$45	$45

ABC's Gym's Earnings

24 sessions	36 sessions	48 sessions
$348	$522	$696

By allowing the client to train with Personal Training Business, Inc. without joining the gym, ABC's Gym is recovering the $199 three month membership fee plus an additional $6.20, $8.97, and $10.35 for 24, 36, and 48 sessions respectively. This payment of $199 gives ABC's Gym a 27% profit over the $155.73 three-month fee (based on a yearly membership fee of $299 down, $26.99 a month).

6 Months

Number of Sessions	48 (minimum)	72	96
Fee per Session	$40	$40	$40

ABC's Gym's Earnings

48 sessions	72 sessions	96 sessions
$624	$936	$1,248

By allowing the client to train with Personal Training Business, Inc. without joining the gym, ABC's Gym is recovering the $349 six month membership fee plus an additional $5.72, $8.15, and $9.36 for 48, 72, and 96 sessions respectively. This payment of $349 gives ABC's Gym a 12% profit over the $311.46 six- month fee (based on a yearly membership fee of $299 down, $26.99 a month).

APPENDIX D

This Personal Training Agreement includes details of various training plans and payment schedules. This is provided only as an example of the issues that should be addressed in a Personal Trainer Agreement.

PERSONAL TRAINING AGREEMENT

THIS PERSONAL TRAINING AGREEMENT, (hereinafter, the "Agreement") is made and entered into this ____day of_____20___, by and between PERSONAL TRAINING BUSINESS, INC., and _____, (hereinafter, the "Client"). PERSONAL TRAINING BUSINESS, INC. and the Client are sometimes collectively referred to in this Agreement as the "Parties."

Where the context requires, the masculine shall be deemed to include the feminine and vice versa; and the singular shall be deemed to include the plural and vice-versa.

Any Client under the age of 18 must have a parent or legal guardian co-sign this Agreement. The Co-signer, along with the Client, agrees to be bound by all the terms and conditions of this Agreement.

As used herein, the term "Activities Under This Agreement" shall mean the following: "testing, including but not limited to testing of the cardiovascular system, heart rate, muscle strength, endurance, and flexibility; training; exercise; aerobics and aerobic conditioning and training; weight training; circuit training; cardiovascular exercise and training; use of machinery, training equipment, free weights, circuit machinery, and cardiovascular machines; stretching; weight lifting; and any other training activities, techniques, and/or exercises."

THE PARTIES HEREBY AGREE TO THE FOLLOWING:

CLIENT HAS READ AND EXECUTED THE "FULL DISCLOSURE OF PHYSICAL CONDITIONS/INFORMED CONSENT AND ASSUMPTION OF THE RISK, AND RELEASE OF LIABILITY," WHICH IS ATTACHED HERETO AND INCORPORATED INTO THIS AGREEMENT AS IF FULLY SET FORTH HEREIN.

PART I   TRAINING PACKAGES AND PAYMENTS

Client acknowledges that he is contracting for the services of a personal trainer provided by PERSONAL TRAINING BUSINESS, INC. A different trainer may be assigned to the Client at any time at the sole discretion of PERSONAL TRAINING BUSINESS, INC.

Each Training Session shall last fifty-five minutes (hereinafter "Training Session"). The Client shall elect one of the following training packages:

ONE-TO-ONE TRAINING PACKAGE

1. A one-to-one training package shall consist of _____ (_____) training sessions ("One-to-One Training Package").

2. The Client agrees to pay PERSONAL TRAINING BUSINESS, INC., the sum of _____dollars ($_____) per One-to-One Training Package, payable as follows:

A. The full sum of _____dollars ($ _____), as stated in Part I (2) above, which sum shall constitute full payment for the first One-to-One Training Package purchased by the Client.

B. If the Client purchases one Training Session at a time, payment per Training Session is due in full prior to the commencement of each Training Session.

C. Payment per One-to-One Training Package is due in full prior to the commencement of the first Training Session in each Training Package.

D. One-to-One Training Packages must be used within (_____) days of their respective effective dates, as defined below.

    1.   The effective date (hereinafter, "Effective Date") for each One-to-One Training Package shall be the date upon which this Agreement is executed by both Parties, in the case of the initial One-to-One Training Package.

    2.   The Effective Date for any subsequently purchased One-to-One Training Packages, after the first One-to-One Training Package, shall be the date of the first Training Session under such subsequently purchased One-to-One Training Packages.

    3.   The Client agrees that any Training Session not used within (____) days of the Effective Date for any One-to-One Training Package shall be forfeited. The Client shall not be entitled to a refund of the cost for any Training Session not used within _____ (_____) days of the Effective Date of any One-to-One Training Package.

E. The amounts payable per One-to-One Training Package and/or Training Session may be adjusted at PERSONAL TRAINING BUSI-NESS, INC.'s sole discretion, at any time. The Client waives notice of any such adjustments to the amounts payable per One-to-One Training Package and/or Training Session.

F. To avoid the loss of the entire Training Session a Training Session must be canceled or rescheduled no later than 5:00 p.m. the previous evening for next morning appointments (5 a.m. - 12 p.m.) and no later than 8:00 a.m. for same afternoon and evening appointments (1 p.m. - 10 p.m.).

    1.   If the Client fails to cancel or reschedule a Training Session as stated in I(2)(F), the cost of the Training Session will not be refunded or applied to any future Training Session, but shall be forfeited by the Client.

G. Should additional Training Sessions be requested, without the purchase of additional One-to-One Training Packages, the Client agrees to pay _____ dollars ($_____) per Training Session, in full prior to the commencement of each additional Training Session.

H. Should the Client purchase additional Training Sessions and/or One-to-One Training Packages, both the Client and PERSONAL TRAINING BUSINESS, INC. agree that this Agreement shall remain in full force and effect, and continue to govern the rights and liabilities of the Parties, except as to the amount payable per such additional Training Session or One-to-One Training Package, if different from the amount stated in I(2), I(2)(A), or I(2)(G) above, or unless the Parties execute a new Agreement.

GOAL ACHIEVEMENT PROGRAM

1. Client elects a minimum ninety (90) day training package ("Goal Achievement Program").

   A. The Goal Achievement Program consists of (_____) Training Sessions per week for a minimum of ninety (90) days.

2. Client shall pay _____ dollars ($_____) for the Goal Achievement Program in full upon the execution of this Agreement; or pay as follows:

   A. The initial payment is _____dollars ($_____), which is due on _____,20_____and is payable by the Client upon execution of this Agreement.

   B. The second payment is _____ dollars ($_____), which is due on _____,20_____and is payable by Electronic Funds Transfer (EFT).

   C. The third payment is _____ dollars ($_____), which is due on _____,20_____and is payable by EFT.

   D. At the end of the ninety (90) day program, the Client's Training Sessions shall either:

       1.   Continue monthly until such time as the Client gives notice as provided in Part II, below. **Client's initials (_____)**.

       2.   Terminate **Client's initials (_____)**.

   E. Client agrees to pay all invoices upon receipt from the Company or from any agent of the Company, and to honor all EFT's until this Agreement is canceled as provided in Part II below.

3. The Client agrees that the Client shall use all ___(___) Training Sessions per week.

   A. If, for any reason, other than the cancellation of a Training Session by the Trainer, all _____ (___) Training Sessions are not used in any given week, the Client forfeits the unused Training Session. The Client shall not be entitled to a refund of the cost for any Training Session not used in any given week.

4. Client expressly agrees that this Agreement shall remain in full force and effect and shall continue to govern the rights and liabilities of the Parties beyond the initial ninety (90) day Goal Achievement Program, and until this Agreement is canceled as provided in Part II below.

PART II   TERMINATION OF AGREEMENT

1. The Client shall have the right to terminate this Agreement upon thirty days (30) advance written notice that the Client is canceling this Agreement to PERSONAL TRAINING BUSINESS, INC., by hand delivery to PERSONAL TRAINING BUSINESS, INC., or by certified mail, return receipt requested to PERSONAL TRAINING BUSINESS, INC., at the Address for Notices as defined in Part IV, below.

A. In the event the Client terminates this Agreement, PERSONAL TRAINING BUSINESS, INC. shall retain all payments made for all unused Training Sessions and/or any unused portion of a One-to-One Training Package or Goal Achievement Program.

2. PERSONAL TRAINING BUSINESS, INC. shall have the right to terminate this Agreement upon fifteen (15) days advance written notice to the Client, hand delivered to the Client, or by certified mail, return receipt requested to the Client's Address for Notices as defined in Part IV, below.

A. In the event PERSONAL TRAINING BUSINESS, INC. terminates this Agreement, PERSONAL TRAINING BUSINESS, INC. shall refund to the Client all payments made for unused portions of a One-to-One Training Package or Goal Achievement Program.

PART III   DEFAULTS

1. If the Client shall fail to perform any of the covenants, conditions, or agreements herein contained to be kept or performed under this Agreement, including but not limited to the payments provided in Part I above, any and all rights of the Client hereunder shall, at the sole option of PERSONAL TRAINING BUSINESS, INC., immediately cease and expire as fully and with like effect as if the entire Agreement herein had terminated by the use of all Training Sessions and/or One-to-One Training Package or Goal Achievement Program. Upon the Client's default, the Client shall forfeit all payments made for all unused Training Sessions and/or any unused portions of a One-to-One Training Package or Goal Achievement Program. The forfeiture of all such payments shall not affect and shall be in addition to any other remedy of PERSONAL TRAINING BUSINESS, INC. under this Agreement, at law, in equity, or by statute.

PART IV   NOTICE ADDRESSES

1. PERSONAL TRAINING BUSINESS, INC.'s Address for Notices:

PERSONAL TRAINING BUSINESS, INC. c/o ABC's Gym 1234 Main Street, Anytown, USA

2. The Client's Address for Notices:

PART V   *FEE FOR BAD CHECK AND COSTS OF ATTORNEY'S FEES*

1. If any of the Client's checks for payments under this contract are returned for insufficient funds on the first presentment, PERSONAL TRAINING BUSINESS, INC. will charge, and the Client agrees to pay, a bad check fee of $15.00. PERSONAL TRAINING BUSINESS, INC. will charge, and the Client agrees to pay, a charge of $15.00 for any electronic funds transfer payments that are not honored for any reason.

2. The Parties agree that The Client shall be liable for PERSONAL TRAINING BUSINESS, INC.'s reasonable attorney's fees incurred in instituting and prosecuting any action or proceeding instituted by reason of any default of the Client under this Agreement with all damages, interest, and costs expended. PERSONAL TRAINING BUSINESS, INC. shall be entitled to interest on any judgment obtained against the Client at the judgment rate of interest as defined in Va. Code Section 6.1-330.54.

PART VI   *HEADINGS*

1. The section headings used in this Agreement are for reference purposes only and shall not in any way affect the meaning or interpretation of this Agreement.

PART VII   *GOVERNING LAW AND WAIVER OF TRIAL BY JURY*

1. This Agreement shall be governed by and construed in accordance with the laws of the Commonwealth of Virginia without regard to conflicts of law. PERSONAL TRAINING BUSINESS, INC. and the Client each agree to and they hereby do waive trial by jury in any action, proceeding, or counterclaim brought by either of the Parties hereto against the other on any matters whatsoever arising out of or in any way connected with this Agreement, the relationship between the Parties under this Agreement, or the Client's participation in the Activities Under This Agreement.

PART VIII   *VALIDITY OF AGREEMENT*

1. If any term or provision of this Agreement is held to be invalid or unenforceable in any respect, such invalidity or unenforceability shall not affect the validity or enforceability of any other term or provision of this Agreement, and this Agreement shall be construed as if such invalid or unenforceable provision or term had never been contained herein.

PART IX WAIVER OR MODIFICATION

1. No modification of this Agreement or of any covenant, condition, or limitation of this Agreement shall be valid unless memorialized in a writing executed by both PERSONAL TRAINING BUSINESS, INC. and the Client. No waiver by PERSONAL TRAINING BUSINESS, INC. of any breach or asserted breach of this Agreement shall constitute a waiver or limitation of PERSONAL TRAINING BUSINESS, INC.'s right to subsequently enforce and compel strict compliance with every provision of this Agreement. Nor shall any waiver by PERSONAL TRAINING BUSINESS, INC. of any breach or asserted breach of this Agreement constitute a waiver or limitation of any continuing, subsequent, or other breach or asserted breach by the Client of the provisions of this Agreement.

PART X ENTIRE AGREEMENT

1. This Agreement (including the Full Disclosure of Physical Conditions/ Informed Consent and Assumption of the Risk and Release of Liability) constitutes the entire agreement of the Parties, and supersedes any and all previous understandings, agreements, arrangements, or discussions, written or oral, between the Parties relating hereto. There are no collateral agreements, representations, or guarantees, oral or otherwise unless attached hereto and signed by both Parties.

NOTICE TO CLIENT

1. Do not sign this Agreement before you have read all pages to this Agreement, because terms on all pages are a part of this Agreement. The Client is entitled to a completely filled-in copy of this Agreement.

2. The Client certifies that he understands and agrees: (1) That this document is a contract that will become legally binding upon the signature of both Parties; (2) To the terms and conditions of this contract; and (3) There are no warranties either express or implied in this Agreement that are not expressly contained in this Agreement.

BY SIGNING BELOW, THE CLIENT CERTIFIES THAT HE OR SHE HAS RECEIVED A COMPLETED COPY OF THIS AGREEMENT AND AGREES TO BE BOUND THEREBY.

PERSONAL TRAINING BUSINESS, INC.

CLIENT SIGN:

CO-SIGNER (IF APPLICABLE)   PRINT:

APPENDIX E

Health History Questionnaire

(This information will remain confidential)

General Information

Name:
Address:
Phone: Home: /   /   Work: /   /
Email:
Date of Birth: /   /
Height: ft.   inches   Weight: lbs
Personal Physician:
        Address:
        Phone: /   /
Person to Contact in Case of Emergency:
        Relation:

Personal Health History

Has a doctor ever told you your blood pressure was too high?	Yes No
Has a doctor ever told you your cholesterol was too high?	Yes No
Has a doctor ever said that you had heart trouble?	Yes No
Have you ever had difficulty breathing?	Yes No
Have you ever had dizziness or fainting spells?	Yes No
Have you ever had chest pains?	Yes No
Have you ever had a heart attack? Date(s):	Yes No
Have you ever had a stroke? Date(s):	Yes No
Do you suffer from any bone/joint problems, such as arthritis and/or tendinitis?	Yes No
Do you suffer from lower back pain syndrome?	Yes No
Are you diabetic?	Yes No
Females: Have youever had a hysterectomy?	Yes No

Please list any other conditions that may prohibit and/or restrict you starting an exercise program:

List any medications you are currently taking:

Smoking History

Have you ever smoked cigarettes, cigars, or pipes?   Yes No
Presently smoking?   packs/day
Last smoked: years/months ago

Nutrition History

What is your current weight?   lbs
What is the heaviest you have ever weighed (excluding pregnancy) ?
                              lbs
Do you consume alcohol?   Yes No
        If yes, how many drinks/week?   _____

How many meals do you eat during the average day?   _____
Have you ever been on a weight reduction program?   Yes No
        Did you achieve your goals?   Yes No
        Permanently?   Yes No
Do you eat at least 1,200 calories a day?   Yes No
Do you consume beverages with caffeine?   Yes No
        If yes, describe:
Number of times per week you usually eat: _____ breakfast
_____lunch   _____dinner   _____snacks
List any vitamins and/or dietary supplements you are currently taking:

Exercise History

Are you currently involved in any aerobic activities
        (e.g., bicycle, treadmill)?   Yes No
        If yes, how many days/week?   _____
        If no, when was the last time such activity was performed?
                             _____ months/years ago
Are you currently involved in any resistance training activities?   Yes No
        If yes, how many days/week?   _____
        If no, when was the last time such activity was performed?
        _____ months/years ago   Never
What other activities, if any, are you currently involved in?

How many days per week do you exercise?
        _____ ; _____minutes/day
Are you interested in getting into a regular exercise program?   Yes No
        If yes, what activities would you prefer (circle):
                walking   running   aerobics
                stairmaster   bicycle   rowing
                free weights   machines

Family History

List all of your immediate family members. Please include their age, health
status, or age at death and the cause:

Has anyone in your immediate family had:
        heart attack under the age of 50   Yes No
        stroke under the age of 50   Yes No
        diabetes   Yes No
        high blood pressure   Yes No
        high cholesterol (>240 mg/dl)   Yes No
        obesity (20 or more pounds overweight)   Yes No
        cancer   Yes No
If you answered yes to any of these please explain:

APPENDIX F

Medical Clearance Form

Your patient, _____ , has applied to participate in One-to-One fitness training with Personal Training Business, Inc., which requires your medical clearance prior to participation. Clearance indicates that this patient has no contraindications for participation in the below-described fitness tests and One-to-One fitness training. The program will include any or all of the following:

1) Health history questionnaire and health screening
2) Resting measures (e.g., heart rate, blood pressure, % body fat, anthropometrics)
3) Muscle strength/endurance assessment
4) Cardiorespiratory assessment
5) Flexibility assessment
6) Fitness program to ensure Functional Capacity

The American College of Sports Medicine (2000) recommends that apparently healthy women over 55 years old and men over 45 years old, who are going to participate in exercise exceeding 60% of their VO_2max, should have a medical examination and/or an exercise test.

Does your patient's risk factor assessment warrant such a medical examination prior to exercise testing? PLEASE CIRCLE ONE: YES   NO

My patient,_____,is physically able to participate in the above-described testing regimen (>60% max VO_2max), and an individually instructed exercise (aerobic and resistance training) program. PLEASE CIRCLE ONE: No considerations   See below

Printed Name: _____ , M.D.

Signature: _____ , M.D.

Address:

Please list any restrictions, contraindications, and/or concerns (including medications). Thank you for your cooperation.

Please fax completed medical clearance form to:

Your Name
Personal Training Business, Inc. - Post Rehab Conditioning Specialists
Office: 555.555.5555 Fax: 555.777.7777

APPENDIX G

Release of Information Form

TO WHOM IT MAY CONCERN:

Please furnish to Personal Training Business, Inc. (hereinafter "Facility") and/or any of its personnel, information, copies of any and all hospital and medical records or reports of any sort, charts, notes, x-rays, lab reports, and prescription information, including the right to inspect and copy such records. Facility is to be furnished any and all other information without limitation pertaining to any confinement, examination, treatment, or condition of myself, including medical, dental, psychological, or other treatment, examinations, or counseling for any condition, medical, dental, or psychological.

This AUTHORIZATION shall be considered as continuing and you may rely upon it in all respects unless you have previously been advised by me in writing to the contrary. It is expressly understood by the undersigned and you are hereby authorized with the same validity as though an original had been presented to you.

Dated this _____ day of _____ , 20 _____

Signature: _____

Name: _____

Address: _____

_____

_____

Phone: H: _____/_____/_____   W: _____/_____/_____

APPENDIX H

Full Disclosure of Physical Conditions / Informed Consent and Assumption of Risk and Release of Liability

This "Full Disclosure of Physical Conditions/Informed Consent and Assumption of the Risk, and Release of Liability" is executed this _____ day of _____, 20____ , and is a material part of, and is incorporated by reference into the Personal Training Agreement executed by the Client and dated the _____ day of _____, 20____ as if fully set forth therein.

1. The Client certifies that he is physically sound and suffering from no condition, impairment, disease, infirmity, or illness that would prevent his participation in the Client's Activities Under This Agreement (as defined on page 1 of the Agreement), except as hereinafter stated. _____ (Client's Initials).

2. The Client certifies that he has been informed of the need for a physician's approval for participation in the Activities Under This Agreement. _____ (Client's Initials).

3. The Client certifies that PERSONAL TRAINING BUSINESS, INC. has recommended that the Client have a yearly or more frequent physical examination and consultation with the Client's physician as to physical activity, exercise, and use of exercise and training equipment so that the Client may have knowledge that he has either (a) been given permission by the Client's physician to participate, or (b) that the Client has decided to participate in the Activities Under This Agreement without the approval of his physician. _____ (Client's Initials).

4. The Client expressly assumes all responsibility for the Client's participation in the Activities Under This Agreement.

5. THE CLIENT CERTIFIES THAT THE CLIENT HAS GIVEN FULL AND COMPLETE DISCLOSURE OF ALL PHYSICAL CONDITIONS, IMPAIRMENTS, DISEASES, INFIRMITIES OR ILLNESSES THAT MIGHT AFFECT OR PREVENT THE CLIENT'S PARTICIPATION IN THE ACTIVITIES UNDER THIS AGREEMENT. THE CLIENT REPRESENTS THAT HE HAS NO CONGENITAL, PHYSICAL, OR MENTAL HEALTH PROBLEMS, NO UNDERLYING CARDIOVASCULAR, NEUROLOGICAL, OR ANY ILLNESS, OR CONDITION WHICH MIGHT AFFECT OR PREVENT THE CLIENT'S PARTICIPATION IN THE ACTIVITIES UNDER THIS AGREEMENT.

INFORMED CONSENT AND ASSUMPTION OF THE RISK

1. The Client enters into this Agreement with full knowledge of all risks and benefits associated with the Activities Under This Agreement. The Client certifies that the Client is of a legal age to enter into a contract, and is not mentally incapacitated. The Client certifies that he enters into this Agreement without duress, undue influence, and for valuable consideration.

2. The Client certifies he understands the risks associated with participation in the Activities Under This Agreement including, but not limited to physical injury resulting from the acts, omissions, and/or negligence of others. The Client certifies that the Client knows and fully understands the importance and relevance of all risks, and expressly and voluntarily assumes any and all risks associated with the Client's participation in the Activities Under This Agreement, including but not limited to the activities of training; exercise; aerobics and aerobic conditioning and training; weight training; circuit training; cardiovascular exercise and training; use of machinery, training equipment, free weights, circuit machinery and cardiovascular machines; stretching; weight lifting; testing, including but not limited to testing of the cardiovascular system, heart rate, muscle strength, endurance, and flexibility; and any other training activities, techniques, and/or exercises. Further, the Client expressly and voluntarily assumes any and all risk associated with the Client's participation in the Activities Under This Agreement, including but not limited to the risks of dizziness; strains and/or sprains; fractures of any kind; syncope (fainting); arrhythmia (alteration in heart rhythm); dyspnea (shortness of breath); angina pectoris (chest pain); tachycardia (rapid resting heart rate over 100 beats per minute); myocardial infarction (heart attack); cerebrovascular accident (stroke); dysrhythmia (abnormal rhythm of brain waves or heart rhythm), and/or any other physical injury, due to any cause whatsoever.

RELEASE OF LIABILITY

1. Client certifies that the Client voluntarily agrees to participate in the Activities Under This Agreement, including but not limited to the activities of training; exercise; aerobics and aerobic conditioning and training; weight training; circuit training; cardiovascular exercise and training; use of machinery, training equipment, free weights, circuit machinery and cardiovascular machines; stretching; weight lifting; testing, including but not limited to testing of the cardiovascular system, heart rate, muscle strength, endurance, and flexibility; and any other training activities, techniques, and/or exercises. The Client further agrees to follow all rules set forth by PERSONAL TRAINING BUSINESS, INC.

2. In consideration of the privilege of participating in the Activities Under This Agreement, and the training services provided by PERSONAL TRAINING BUSINESS, INC. the Client for himself, his heirs, assigns, administrators, executors, and/or all members of his family, including minors, waives, releases, holds harmless and forever discharges PERSONAL TRAINING BUSINESS, INC., its successors in interest, assigns, servants, agents, employees, independent contractors, associates, officers, directors, officials and any other participants in the Activities Under This Agreement, from any and all responsibility, liability, claims and demands of any kind and nature, damages, actions, causes of action of any kind, whether now known or unknown, or which the Client may have now, or which may hereafter accrue to the Client (collectively, the "Claims"), including but not limited to Claims based upon or related to dizziness; strains and/or sprains; fractures of any kind; syncope (fainting); arrhythmia (alteration in heart rhythm); dyspnea (shortness of breath); angina pectoris (chest pain); tachycardia (rapid resting heart rate over 100 beats per minute); myocardial infarction (heart attack); cerebrovascular accident (stroke); dysrhythmia (abnormal rhythm of brain waves or heart rhythm); and/or any other physical injury, due to any cause whatsoever, including the act or omission, negligence or any other fault of PERSONAL TRAINING BUSINESS, INC., its successors in interest, assigns, servants, agents, employees, independent contractors, associates, officers, directors, officials and any other participants in the Activities Under This Agreement.

PERSONAL TRAINING BUSINESS, INC.

PRINTED NAME: BY:

SIGNATURE: TITLE:

CO-SIGNER (IF APPLICABLE):

APPENDIX I

Policy and Procedure Manual

1. Trainers must annually accrue Continuing Education Credits (CEUs). A minimum of ten (10) lecture hours by an accredited association or organization must be performed or their employment status may be subject to review and/or termination.

2. Proper professional attire is required while training clients. In accordance with maintaining a professional image the following is recommended:

    a. Professional personal trainers shirt

    b. Long black athletic pants (winter)

    Black athletic shorts (summer)

    c. Uniform must be tucked in and neat

    d. Socks, with an ankle, should be worn.

    e. Athletic sneakers must be worn- preferably with white as the majority color.

    f. Baseball caps, or hats of any kind, may not be worn.

3. Trainers are to treat clients in a professional and ethical manner.

4. Trainers must be punctual for scheduled appointments.

5. Trainers must ensure that their clients sign in the Personal Trainers Log Book. Payments for incomplete logging will be withheld until completed in a satisfactory manner. Information needed every time a client trains consists of the following:

    a. Client's printed name

    b. Time of training session

    c. Number of sessions purchased or type of training package

    d. Current training session number

    e. Client's initials

    f. Initials of a witness

6. Completed contracts must be placed in the Director of Training's mailbox for review and signature. Included with any new contract should be a photocopied completed Health History Questionnaire, Fitness Consultation Form, Fitness Evaluation, Full Disclosure of Physical Conditions/Informed Consent and Assumption of Risk and Release of Liability, Physician's Release (if necessary), Payment Control Sheet, and any other information relating to the client, must be attached with the completed contract. Commission payment may be withheld if

contracts are not completed in full and/or any of the other aforementioned materials relating to a new client are missing.

7. Follow-up postcards are to be sent to every individual following a Fitness Consultation regardless of whether they signed up for personal training. These postcards are then placed in the Director of Training's mailbox.

8. Fitness Consultation forms are to be filled out completely. Forms with clients interested in personal training (those interested that have not signed up) are to be placed in the Director of Training's mailbox, with a note describing the prospects interests in personal training. All other fitness consultation forms are to be placed in the Completed Fitness Consultation Box.

9. Trainers are to send postcards to their clients on a monthly basis highlighting some aspect of their progress and/or fitness training. Postcards are to be placed in the Director of Training's mailbox.

10. Trainers are responsible for keeping track of their clients' Fitness Evaluation re-testing dates. Though the trainer assessing the Fitness Evaluation is also responsible for these dates, such a practice will ensure timely re-testing sessions with clients. Trainers are required to send their clients re-testing postcards a minimum of one (1) week prior to the re-testing date.

11. Trainers will keep outside conversations with trainers, gym members, and/or friends to a bare minimum while training a client on the "client's time."

12. Trainers must take showers if they will be training clients immediately following their own workouts.

13. Gum and/or mints are permitted as long as the usage of these materials remains discreet.

14. Trainer is required to attend monthly staff meetings. With proper written notice and explanation, a trainer may miss a required staff meeting. In addition to a monthly staff meeting, trainers may be required to be present for other activities defined by Personal Training Business, Inc. (lectures, health fairs, speaking engagements, etc.). Trainers will be given suf-ficient notice prior to any such activities.

15. Trainers are solely responsible for maintaining, and paying for, current personal training certification(s), and Cardiopulmonary Resuscitation (CPR) certification.

16. Payroll sheets are due no later than the second day of each month. Incomplete and/or incorrect invoices can and will delay payments due.

17. Trainers are to treat all health club members (clients and non-clients) in a professional and ethical manner.

18. Trainer agrees to keep all information regarding their clientele confidential.

19. Trainers agree to create a safe atmosphere when working with their clients. In an attempt to minimize the risk of injury to the client, the trainer agrees not to have the client lift weights any faster than four (4) seconds on the lowering (eccentric) phase and two (2) seconds on the up (concentric) phase. Furthermore, the trainer will ensure that the client never racks or de-racks the weights during any and all training sessions while under the services of said trainer.

20. Trainer agrees to avoid any exercises that may put his client at risk of injury.

21. All inquiries regarding personal training, fitness consultations, fitness evaluations, and/or training sessions must be responded to within twenty-four (24) hours. In addition, trainer must notify the Director of Training (in writing or voice mail) of the result of said inquiries within same twenty-four (24) hour period. Such procedure ensures that the trainer provides a high quality of service to the prospect/client(s).

22. Trainer agrees to send prospect/client(s) letters and/or postcards for the prospect's / client's birthdays.

23. All training practices incorporated by trainers must have the client's satisfaction as the number one objective.

24. Trainer agrees to follow all [Your Company Name] Personal Training and Kinesiology Procedures set forth in [Your Company Name] Code of Conduct and Policy Manual.

25. [Your Company Name] is not responsible for *any* payments to trainer for personal training sessions which have expired (per clients' agreements).

26. It is recommended that trainers have a pager (with voicemail) so correspondence with the Director of Training and other trainers is expedited.

27. Trainers are to send a minimum of ten (10) postcards to past clients inquiring about their current workouts, or any other health and/or fitness related topic. These postcards are to be placed in the Director of Training's mailbox.

I, _____ (print name) have read and understand the "[Your Company Name] Code of Conduct Policy Manual" set forth herein by [Your Company Name} and agree to follow said policies and procedures.

Signature   Date

[Your Name]   Date   [Your Company Name}

APPENDIX J

Sample Press Release

CONTACT: Your Name
            Office: 555.555.5555 Voice: 555.555.5555

FOR IMMEDIATE RELEASE

Personal Training Business' Runners Training Program Helping Raise Money for Multiple Sclerosis

Tyson's Corner, VA — The Personal Training Business' Runners Training Program is a charity-oriented program geared toward preparing runners to complete the seventh annual MS Challenge 1/2 Marathon on September 19, 2001. Personal Training Business, with presenting sponsor Company Name of Anytown, USA, is targeting their Runners Training Program to novice and intermediate runners. This 13-week program includes weekly runs with veteran marathoners and certified strength and conditioning experts, informative seminars on nutrition, injury prevention, proper running attire and footwear, and MORE!

Multiple Sclerosis is one of the most common neurological diseases affecting young adults. Unfortunately, there is no known cause or cure. With the help of its Training Program participants, Personal Training Business will raise money for the National Multiple Sclerosis Society. All monies raised will go toward MS research.

Your Name, president and founder, states "Personal Training Business has always been committed to helping people meet their fitness needs. Now we can help runners achieve their goal of completing a half-marathon AND raise money for MS."

Personal Training Business' Runners Training Program is hosting "Informational Orientations" at ABC's Gym, Anytown on June 12th at 9 a.m. and June 16th at 8:30 p.m. For more information, or to reserve your space, call 555.555.5555 today!

APPENDIX K

Summer Promotion

Friends Workout for Free in June!

Dear Valued Client,

Beach season is almost upon us. As a client of Personal Training Business, Inc., you are currently working hard to reach your fitness goals. Your friends, however, may not be so lucky. For some, the winter months prove to be a breeding ground for unwanted weight gain. Do you know anyone who may benefit from losing a few unwanted pounds? Help your friends learn how to exercise correctly and shed their winter weight in time for summer.

During the month of June, we will offer a **FREE** personal training session to any family member, friend, and/or co-worker who wants to improve the quality of their life.

Let those you care about most see firsthand the results possible by being active. We look forward to your taking advantage of this great opportunity.

Best of health,

Your Name
Director of Training

APPENDIX L

Winter Promotion

Give the Gift of Fitness!

Dear Valued Client,

This holiday season, when you are shopping for the perfect gift for your family or friends, think about giving the "Gift of Fitness." Personal Training Business Gift Certificates make great gifts. They help family and/or friends live a better lifestyle, while also endorsing the benefits of being active. Whether someone you care about needs a few sessions to get started, or one-to-one attention for a more substantial period of time, Personal Training Business has gift certificates to meet their needs.

Let those you care about most see firsthand the results possible by being active. This holiday season give the gift of fitness. For information on purchasing gift certificates, please call our office at 555.555.5555.

Happy Holidays,

Your Name
Director of Training

APPENDIX M

Sample Thank You Letter

Dear   ·   :

It is gratifying to know that you have chosen Personal Training Business personal training services. If you have any questions regarding your fitness program, or if you have general questions or thoughts, please don't hesitate to call. We would like to be of assistance any way we can. One of Personal Training Business' highest priorities is to ensure that you are a satisfied client.

As you may know, the majority of our business comes from referrals by satisfied clients like yourself. If you know of anyone who might benefit from our services, we would greatly appreciate you telling them about Personal Training Business. Enclosed please find Gift Certificates for FREE fitness consultations for friends, family, and/or co-workers.

Thank you once again for choosing Personal Training Business.

Best of health,

Personal Training Business Personal Training Staff

APPENDIX N

Client Checklist and Retention Procedures

Trainer:

Start Date: End Date:

Continue Monthly: Yes   No

Source of Client: _____

                Add name to Front Desk Commission folder (if necessary)

Client Name:

Address: _____

           street

_____

           city/town, state, zip code

Phone: H)_____/_____/_____   W)_____/_____/_____

Date of Birth: _____/_____/_____

Type of Personal Training Package:

Trainer has obtained each of the following documents and has left all

           originals in Director of Training's box to sign:

                (Please check the appropriate boxes)

___ Personal Training Agreement

___ Informed Consent

___ EFT form with a copy of voided check or charge slip

___ Health History Questionnaire

___ Fitness Consultation Form

___ New Client Information Sheet

___ Payment Control Sheet

New Client Procedures

Personal Trainer

      ___ "Thank you for choosing Personal Training Business" postcard
has been written and placed in The Director of Training's "To
be mailed" box.

         Date performed:

___ Phone call day after first workout.
> Date performed:

Re-Testing dates:
> ___ 3 months from start date:
> ___ 9 months from start date:
> ___ 15 months from start date:
> ___ Trainer has given client a T-shirt/tank top (depending on supply)
> Date performed:

Director of Training
> ___ "Thank you for choosing Personal Training Business" letter sent
> Date performed:
> ___ Has put client address in computer under "Client's Mailing
> Address" and in Excel Mailing List
> Date performed:
> ___ Has sent a subscription to *ACE FitnessMatters*
> Date performed:

Retention Procedures

Personal Trainer
> ___ Birthday postcard sent (Trainer) (placed in Director of Training's
> box)
> Date performed:
> ___ Monthly postcard (various topics—12 sent annually) (Director's
> box)
> Dates performed:

> ___ Postcard sent asking for referrals.
> Date performed:
> ___ Holiday card sent (Director of Training's box)
> Date performed:

___ List clients with NEW addresses (name and address):

___ Postcard sent when client leaves Personal Training Business
    Date performed:

___ Other (explain):
    Date performed:

Personal Trainer- Quarterly (Jan.1, April 1, July 1, Oct.1)

___ Send Former Client postcard inquiring about current workouts, etc.
    Date performed:

Director of Training

___ Phone call regarding quality of training service
    Date performed:

___ Letter to client's physician regarding program
    Date performed:

___ Sent client copy of Fitness Evaluation with cover letter (if necessary) Date performed:

___ Questionnaire regarding trainer's quality of service sent
    Date performed:

___ Thanks for Questionnaire (if necessary)
    Date performed:

___ Request for a Testimonial
    Date performed:

___ Thanks for Testimonial
    Date performed:

___ Birthday postcard sent
    Date performed:

___ Holiday card sent
    Date performed:

___ Thanks for choosing Personal Training Business (Client leaving)
    Date performed:

APPENDIX O

Checklist of Required Items for New Site

___ Computer
___ Software for computer (e.g. Microsoft Office)
___ Transference of hard-drive information to new computer
___ Printer
___ Phone line (health club line or separate business line installed)
___ Answering service or machine
___ File cabinet (4 or 5 drawers high) stocked for opening day
___ Desk
___ Chair for desk
___ Stacking Mailboxes (for Trainers, for To Do items, for To Be Filed Items, To Be Paid items, etc.)
___ Chair(s), bench, or love seat for clients
___ Certifications (for hanging)
___ Frames for certifications (hung on wall)
___ Company Personal Training Manual (several copies)
___ Company Personal Training Exam (several copies)
___ Company Code of Conduct and Policy Manual
___ Contractor Agreements (both types)
___ Calipers (body fat)
___ Measuring Tape
___ Stethoscope and Sphygmomanometer (blood pressure)
___ Medicine Balls (variety of sizes)
___ Elastic Tubing (with handles—at least three different tensions)
___ Sit and Reach Flexibility Tester
___ Hanging File Folders
___ Manila Folders
___ Pens and Pencils
___ Stapler
___ Paper Clips
___ Bookshelf
___ Polaroid Camera (with film)
___ Hanging File Folders and Copies for the following:
   ___ New client information sheets
   ___ Personal Training agreements
   ___ Request for Pre-Authorized Payment Program
   ___ Release of Liability Forms
   ___ Health History Questionnaire
   ___ Fitness Consultation Forms
   ___ Client Retention Forms
   ___ Fitness Evaluation Forms (trainer's copy)

___ Health and Fitness Evaluation (client's mailed copy)
___ Medical Clearance Forms
___ Payroll Sheets (both types)
___ Blank Daily Sales Control (DSC) Sheets
___ Blank Workout Sheets
___ Monthly Commission Reports (blank)
___ Monthly Sales Control (blank)
___ Price Lists (on/off-site)
___ Personal Training Gift Certificate Form Letters (ABC's Gym members)
___ Free Fitness Consultation Forms (new ABC's members)
___ Questionnaires- Company's clients (blank)
___ Questionnaires- ABC's Gym members (blank)
___ Office "To Do" List (weekly list)
___ Personal Trainer Weekly To Do List
___ Personal Trainer Achievement Sheet
___ Interview Question Sheets
___ "Thank you for inquiry" form letters (sent to person's home; must be an Original, not a photocopy version)
___ Payment Control Sheet
___ Fax Sheets
___ Front Desk Personal Training Journal sheets
___ Waiver and Release Form (usage of name and testimonial)
___ Fitness Evaluation Sheets:
___ Standardized Scores (copies)
___ Treadmill Fit Test Program Guidelines
___ Sit and Reach Test Guidelines and information
___ Repetition Maximum Percentage (%) Scores

___ Printed business supplies on hand (before opening day):
___ Envelopes
___ Business cards
___ Brochures
___ Postcards
___ Gift Certificates (postcard size)

___ Company Information Packets:
___ Black Folders
___ Company stickers with Logo
___ Corporate Mission and Philosophy page
___ A Brief Introduction
___ *ACE FitnessMatters*
___ Copies of published article(s)
___ Testimonial(s)
___ Price sheets (on-site, off-site)

___ Manila envelopes for the following Vendors/Agencies
    ___ American Council on Exercise (ACE)
    ___ Company's Financial Service
    ___ Continuing Education Credits (CEC's)
    ___ County Information (where company conducts business)
    ___ Screen Printing and Embroidery Company
    ___ Printing Company
    ___ Internal Revenue Service (IRS)
    ___ Insurance Company
    ___ Merchant Account Company
    ___ Company Payroll Services
    ___ State Employment Commission Information

Checklist of Secondary Items

___ Company Logo and Information put on office door

___ Two (2) Banners with Company Logo (hang in office and health club)

___ Framed pictures of "star" clients (athletes, success stories, etc.)

___ Testimonial Board

___ Exercise of the Month board

___ T-shirts, hats, and/or tank tops in stock

___ Lamp (if necessary)

___ Plant (if desired)

___ Mirror

APPENDIX P

Fitness Consultation Form

DATE:

TRAINER:

SOURCE:

ABC's Gym/Initial

Session

Referral:

Advertisement

Other:

Name:

Address:

Phone: H)

      W)

Email:

Date of Birth:

Current Body Weight (lbs):

RISK FACTOR ASSESSMENT

Has a doctor ever told you your blood pressure was too high?	Yes No
Has a doctor ever told you your cholesterol was too high?	Yes No
Has a doctor ever diagnosed you with a heart arrythmia (abnormal heart beat or heart murmur)?	Yes No
Have you ever had difficulty breathing (asthmatic)?	Yes No
Have you ever had dizziness or fainting spells?	Yes No
Have you ever had chest pains?	Yes No
Have you ever had a heart attack? Date(s):	Yes No
Do you suffer from any bone/joint problems (arthritis/tendinitis)?	Yes No
Do you suffer from lower back pain syndrome?	Yes No
Are you diabetic? Yes No Which type? Type 1 Type 2	

CONSULTATION QUESTIONS

When is the last time you have engaged in regular exercise
(>3 times/wk)?

If currently exercising: What type of exercise do you
currently enjoy?

Do you feel comfortable with all the equipment in the gym?   Yes No

      If No: Cardiovascular equipment

          Machines

          Free Weights

          Specific:

If not currently exercising: Why are you beginning an exercise
program at this time?

What motivates you to exercise?

What are your long-term and short-term goals?

How much time (days/week and hours) can you devote towards
realizing these goals?

What support do you have to change your lifestyle?

How will you integrate exercise into your life?

What could derail your fitness program?

Do you have friends who exercise regularly? Are they members
of the gym?

How do you learn best?

When was the last time you had a complete physical examination?

Have you ever had a personal trainer?   Yes No

      If YES: How long ago?

      How long did you work with him/her?

      What results, if any, did you achieve?

      When did you start seeing your personal trainer?

In what ways do you think working with a personal trainer will improve your level of fitness?

If we could show you how you can achieve your aforementioned goals by working with a personal trainer beyond your free sessions, would you be interested?

To Be Completed By Trainer:

Sign up: Yes   What type:
                  No   If no, why:

Next appointment scheduled?   Yes   No
Is a Medical Release required?   Yes   Explain: No
Postcard Sent: Yes   No   Date Sent:
IS PROSPECT INTERESTED IN HIRING A PERSONAL TRAINER?
                                     Yes   No

Trainer's notes:

Office Use Only: Administrator's Initials:
Is fitness consultation form complete?
                                     Yes   No   If no, what is missing?

Postcard/Letter Sent (BDI):   Yes   No   Date:
Follow-up: Initials:
     Phone Call: Yes   No   Date:
     Postcard: Yes   No   Date:

APPENDIX Q

New Client Information Sheet

Date signed: Trainer:

Name:

Address:

E-mail:

Phone: H)

    W)

Date of Birth:

Emergency Contact:

    Name:

    Phone:

    Relationship:

Training Package Information

Package Type:

APPENDIX R

REQUEST FOR PRE-AUTHORIZED PAYMENT PROGRAM

I , _____ , wish to make my payments to Belmont Financial Services, Inc. through its Pre-Authorized Payment Program. I hereby authorize my bank or credit card company to make my payment by the method indicated below and post it to my account.

      CHECKING
      (NOTE: For checking account authorization, attach a voided
check)

      Master Card   Visa

      Account Number: _____
      (A voided imprinted charge ticket must be used)

      Expiration Date: _____/_____/_____

I understand that I am in full control of my payment, and if, at any time, I decide to make any changes or discontinue the Electronic Funds Transfer (EFT) service, I will call or write the above named company. Change of payment method will not affect other provisions and terms of my Personal Training Agreement. All billing changes require 15 days notice to Financial Services, P.O. Box 1, Anytown, USA, 555.555.5555, fax 555.777.7777.

_____

Signature of Account Holder   Date

APPENDIX S

Payment Control Sheet

COLLECTED BY: TRAINER:

CLIENT NAME:

DATE: PACKAGE PURCHASED:

AMOUNT COLLECTED: $

E.F.T. AMOUNT: $ N/A

RENEWING CLIENT: YES   NO   N/A

FORM OF PAYMENT: CHECK   CHECK #:   CASH

     VISA   ACCOUNT#:

                     Exp.

     MASTER CARD   ACCOUNT#:

                     Exp.

     OTHER (MONEY ORDER, AMERICAN EXPRESS, ETC.)

SALES RECEIPT: #

Attach copy of sales receipt, with payment, to this form and place in Director's mailbox

APPENDIX T

Fitness Evaluation

DATE: TRAINER'S NAME:

CLIENT:

TEST: #   HEIGHT: (inches)

AGE:

GIRTH MEASURMENTS   **BODY FAT MEASUREMENTS**

ARM: BICEP: AVG:

CHEST: TRICEP: AVG:

WAIST: SUPRAILLIUM: AVG:

HIPS: SUBSCAPULAR: AVG:

THIGH: TOTAL:

CALF: BODY FAT: (%)

                                 LBM: (lbs.)

                                 FAT: (lbs.)

BODY WEIGHT: (lbs.) BLOOD PRESSURE: /

RESTING HEART RATE:

FLEXIBILITY: (inches)

FIT TEST   **STRENGTH TESTS**

SPEED: (MPH) LEG PRESS: x   (lbs)   1RM=   Ratio=

MHR: BENCH PRESS: x   (lbs)   1RM=   Ratio=

SCORE: PUSH-UPS:

                SIT-UPS:

AEROBIC TRAINING ZONE   **WAIST-HIP**

KARVONEN FORMULA   WAIST=

60%=   HIP=

80%=   RATIO=

APPENDIX U

Fitness Services Menu

PLAN A:

GOAL ACHIEVEMENT PROGRAM (for a duration of 3 months)

Package	# of sessions	Rate	Price/month	Discount
FIT 1	2/week	36	$288.00	$216.00
FIT 2	3/week	34	$408.00	$396.00
FIT 3	4/week	32	$512.00	$624.00

PLAN B:

ONE-TO-ONE TRAINING

Package	# of sessions	Rate	Price	Discount
SOLO 1	5 (30 day exp.)	45	$225.00	
SOLO 2	10 (60 day exp.)	40	$400.00	$50.00

PLAN C:

GROUP APPROACH (price reflects a group of 2 persons)

Package	# of sessions	Rate	Price	Discount
Goal Achievement	N/A	N/A	N/A	25% OFF/person
One-To-One	N/A	N/A	N/A	25% OFF/person

PLAN D:

FITNESS EVALUATION
When purchased as sole service- $59.95
When purchased with a training package- $49.95 ($10.00 savings)

PAYMENT METHODS: Cash, Check, or Credit Card (Visa / MasterCard)
DIRECTOR OF TRAINING: Add $10.00 to above pricing schedule

Home Fitness Services Menu

PLAN A:

THE GOAL ACHIEVEMENT SERVICES (for a duration of 3 months)

Package	# of sessions	Rate	Price/month	Discount
HOME 1	2/week	60	$480.00	$240.00
HOME 2	3/week	55	$660.00	$540.00
HOME 3	4/week	50	$800.00	$960.00

PLAN B:

ONE-TO-ONE SERVICES

Package	# of sessions	Rate	Price	Discount
SOLO 3	5 (30 day exp.)	70	$350.00	
SOLO 4	10 (60 day exp.)	65	$650.00	$50.00

PLAN C:

THE GROUP APPROACH (price reflects a group of 2 persons)

Package	# of sessions	Rate	Price	Discount
Goal Achievement	N/A	N/A	N/A	25% OFF/person
One-To-One	N/A	N/A	N/A	25% OFF/person

PLAN D:

FITNESS EVALUATION SERVICES
When purchased as sole service- $69.95
When purchased with a training package- $59.95 ($10.00 savings)

PAYMENT METHODS: Cash, Check, Credit Card (MasterCard / Visa)
DIRECTOR OF TRAINING: ADD $15.00 TO ABOVE PRICING SCHEDULE

APPENDIX V

Personal Trainer Weekly To-Do List

To be prepared and placed in Director's mailbox no later than WEDNESDAY of each week

Trainer: Week of:

Review of Client Checklist and Retention Forms:
____ Forms are *complete* and have been *updated* (if necessary).
____ Monthly postcards written to *all current clients* (if end of the month)
      N/A ____
____ Each pay period attach completed, original "Personal Trainer Achieve-ment Sheet."
      N/A ____
____ Quarterly (Jan.1, April 1, July 1, Oct.1) send postcards to former clients (re: current workouts, etc.)
____ Quarterly (Jan.1, April 1, July 1, Oct.1) write a health-and-fitness related article to be posted in ABC's Gym. Must be given to Director of Training on floppy disk (Macintosh format preferred)
      N/A ____
____ Attach Retention forms (plus postcards) of clients recently leaving BDI to this "Weekly to do list."
      N/A ____   List names here:
____ List clients with NEW addresses (name and address):

      N/A ____
____ Attach Personal Trainer Achievement sheet (only last week of each month)
      N/A ____
____ Please list any clients (name, address, and the special event) that have had, or will be having, a special event occur in their life (e.g., birth of a child, job promotion, completion of a degree, moving).

____ Postcard placed in Director's mailbox   N/A ____
____ Please list all Fitness Consultations which were conducted during previous week (with comments/outcome):   N/A ____
      Prospect's Name:
      Outcome:

      Prospect's Name:
      Outcome:

      Prospect's Name:
      Outcome:

____ Please call five (5) past "fitness consultations" that met with ABC's instructors that did not opt for personal training. Get update on how their program is going (past consultation forms are located in downstairs file cabinet):

Prospect's Name and Phone Number:
Outcome:

Prospect's Name and Phone Number:
Outcome:

Prospect's Name and Phone Number:
Outcome:

Prospect's Name and Phone Number:
Outcome:

Prospect's Name and Phone Number:
Outcome:

Please list any comments regarding Personal Training Business, Inc. personal training services, your clients, concerns, or input that may help improve the quality of the personal training service we offer:

Index

About the Author

Craig S. Mastrangelo, M.S., President and Founder of The Body Defined, Inc., has been involved in health and fitness for over 10 years. He has a master's degree in exercise science and health from George Mason University. Mr. Mastrangelo has been nationally certified by four personal training agencies, has served as an exam tester for the National Sports Performance Association (NSPA), and has been the strength and conditioning coach to several Olympic athletes.

Mr. Mastrangelo is the event organizer of The Body Defined Runners Training Program, an annual half-marathon training program that helps raise money for the National Multiple Sclerosis Society. In addition, Mr. Mastrangelo has published numerous articles relating to health and fitness, has been quoted in news articles in the *Washington Post* and the *Reston Times*, and has served as a guest fitness expert on the radio (Washington, D.C.).